memoirs of an
AFRICAN POET

a poetry collection by
Kota J. Franklin

TATE PUBLISHING
AND ENTERPRISES, LLC

Published by Tate Publishing & Enterprises, LLC
127 E. Trade Center Terrace | Mustang, Oklahoma 73064 USA
1.888.361.9473 | www.tatepublishing.com

Tate Publishing is committed to excellence in the publishing industry. The company reflects the philosophy established by the founders, based on Psalm 68:11,
"The Lord gave the word and great was the company of those who published it."

Book design copyright © 2016 by Tate Publishing, LLC. All rights reserved.
Cover design by Albert Ceasar Compay
Interior design by Gram Telen

Published in the United States of America

ISBN: 978-1-61739-735-6
1. Poetry / American / African American
2. Poetry / General
16.06.20

Love and Heartbreak Stains You

See through me,
speak my unspoken words,
share with me,
this unbearable pain I feel,
dream with me
the most beautiful of dreams
about life and love,
fantasize with me
the fantasy of sex and fairytales
that roams about my head,
cry with me
the tears of hope, joy, and pain,
live with me,
this life of fortunate and unfortunate events,
breathe with me
this unexplainable, but divine air
that flows through my lungs, and
sing with me
beautiful tunes of peace and harmony, but

why must I write a diary
when there are millions of ears
to confide in?

(Kota J. Franklin)

The poets are only the interpreters of the gods.

—Socrates

Also by Kota J. Franklin

My Heart's Confined Words

To my Nana Teresa
for bringing forth Helena
who gave birth to me.
I love you both, dearly.

Acknowledgments

This dream wouldn't be a reality without the unconditional help of the following invaluable individuals:

Valerie, Anniyah and Keara Franklin, and Damien M. Glasby.

Mrs. Helena Franklin, my best friend and mother. Mr. David K. Franklin, my father.

Wilson, Francis, Kokulo, Yassah, Marzey, Delcina, and David K. Franklin Jr., my brothers and sisters.

Dwain Lyons, Henry J. Martin, Samuel R. Shockley, and Eric Marenco, my comrades.

Thank you all for your support!

A special thank-you to my brother-in-law and friend, Mr. Brian K. Martens, whose friendship welcomed me into the United States. Your friendship, loyalty, prayers, and unconditional love showed me what true friends are really made of. You're loved by me, and despite our differences, nothing shall come between us. God bless you!

Thanks to the almighty God for giving me life, strength, and wisdom!

Contents

Part 2
But the Past Shall Remain the Past!

Part 3
With Special Dedication 2 You!

Only if Life Were Color-Blind!

Part 5
It's Just Life, Not a Just Life, but It's My Life!

Part 6
The Alpha and Omega,
the Beginning and the End,
the King of Kings

Part 7
Bible Verses that Got Me through Combat

Introduction

So long ago I began a journey. I know not where it leads me, but I must stride and travel to rid myself of these words, memories, and discomfort in order to endow my mind with peace.

As many may oppose some of what I write about—stating that things of such exist not in our days—I shall speak with a free mind to expose the love and pain.

Love is and will always be an emotion that we find amongst ourselves and write about today; hate and race will never cease to be a reality whether done secretly or publicly. And these are two of the many things that I've written about herein.

> "Counsel is mine, and sound wisdom: I am understanding; I have strength."
>
> Proverbs 8:14

Part 1

Just Like a Tattoo

Dear Diary,

How do you tell a woman
whom you love so very much
that you've grown apart from her?
How do you let her go
without letting her fall?
How do you make her understand
that sometimes the love that seems a lifetime
is only meant to be seasonal?

Sincerely,
Me

◇◇◇◇◇◇◇◇◇◇

When I was young and began to mature, I always heard the neighbors and older kids at school speak of love in such a great way. It was said to be a place where two souls are intertwined happily, sharing thoughts as though they were telepathists. But it was never told to me how badly it hurt whenever it got sour or simply ended with good-byes. But of course maybe I wasn't listening to that aspect of it, because I too wanted to experience love. The poem that follows talks about the first time I experienced love and the after effects that have accompanied me all my life. I've lived with this because I do believe that love is a good thing, maybe perhaps the greatest of things, and no good thing ever dies.

My Only Tattoo

(2 my first time/love)

I couldn't be seen
without you,
skinned so deep,
your love covered my body
whether naked or clothed.
You matched me,
despite the color I wore;
purple, blue, black, or pink,
your love detailed me
as if clearly written in ink.
It's been so long
since you've been gone,
sweet dreams are no more, and
now reality gives me
the desire to think
about life
and how complete it was
when you and I were *we*.
I miss you.

Is It a Crime?

(2 a crush)

Is it a crime
that I grin when in your presence,
hypnotized by your especially sweet fragrance?

Is it a crime
to speak of you in beautiful tones,
telling of you as my heart's blues,
an Aphrodite?

Is it a crime
that I'm addicted to you,
your aphrodisiacal attributes,
a fulfillment of my sexual desires?

Is it a crime
to wanna please you forever and a day,
to surpass all mortals
even if tomorrow will never pass my way?

Is it a crime
to be impervious to your flaws, weight, or height,
because life isn't always perfect, and
true beauty isn't perfection?

My Love,
is it a crime?

A Voice Message: Push Play

(2 whom it may concern)

I want 2 know U
better than what U portray;
I want 2 see the truth
just like the sincerity of words spoken when I pray.

I want 2 touch U
deeper than how sex can feel.
I want 2 complete U
just like to a starving man, a happy meal.

I want 2 dream of U
smiling through my scariest nightmares.
I want 2 fulfill all of U
just like to a wounded soldier, urgent care.

I want 2 give U hope
just like the restoration of life to the comatose.
I want 2 endeavor with U
through the rest of life and death.

I want 2 do it all,
give my all, so
please pick up the phone, and
just give me a call.

1-(800) I LUV YOU

I'll be waiting!

A Love Untold

Desperation
lies dead in your eyes,
vulnerable as today's generation,
brightening, tempting, beautiful as the sunrise.

Fear
is heard clearly in your speech,
spoken quietly for an ear to hear,
to give Love another chance, you've beseeched.

But somewhere in this world,
your heart in loneliness peacefully dwells,
while betrayal haunts where it trod, because
if Happy were U and I, our lives as One will indeed excel!

In My Search for Sanity (Iraq '07–'08)

(thinking of Her)

At dusk
when the crow crows,
I scream a name in my head
that only my Lord knows.
When spoken,
its sound
is embellished with grace,
my soul's turmoil
is seized by endorphins,
my heart's anguish
is seized by spiritual peace.
So dear to my life
as life itself ought to be,
for as long as I may live,
this name
shall always remain a secret,
just to me!

When U Leave

When U leave,
my heart is reminded of these:
hopeless dreams,
unfaithful memories,
beautiful love stories untold,
solitary love,
abandonment, and
so I fall apart!

> "Beauty as we feel it is something indescribable;
> what it is or what it means can never be said."
>
> George Santayana

When I Look at You

I see beauty,
so fine and exceptionally pure,
beyond the sunset at
Africa's
oceans and lagoons,
across the mighty seas' shores.
I see Intelligence
so knowledgeable and well learnt,
beyond the classes and philosophies of Socrates,
higher than the minds of Immortal Deities.

Just One More Time

(the girl on 108th St.)

I'm burdened with memories of your spirit,
so *amber*,
most precious and shinier than gold.
I see U through the dark skies,
deigning to kiss my lips
before dawn awakens me by surprise.
I've dreamt of U both day and night
hoping to liven our emotions
of this once long ago shared Romance, so
that I'd make love to U
just one more time.

Lonely Like Air

I wander in despair,
lonely like air
surrounding,
flowing
through everyone,
hoping
anyone,
someone,
cares.

◇◇◇◇◇◇◇◇◇◇

He/She says:

"Honey, you've changed a great deal, and things aren't the same with us anymore. You act differently around me as though you're tired of us. What have I done wrong, or did I do anything wrong? You don't seem interested anymore."

She/He says:

"No, honey, it isn't you. I've just been busy lately and thinking a lot. Everything is still the same and my love hasn't and will never change."

I say:

I know everyone has had this conversation at least one or twice in their lives because sometimes after being with someone for so long, love turns out to be a routine. The kiss on the cheek before work, the kiss on the cheek at night before bed. Everything turns out to be done the same, and, sometimes, perhaps boring. So once in a while, your soul yearns for love. You want to hear him/her say, "I love you." You want to go back to the first day you both met, the good times that were shared. The poems that follow show that feeling and express that need.

Tell Me

Tell me
you are real,
let your words
adorn me like jewels.
Tell me
that I'm yours,
let your words
fill me with butterflies, and
chill my spine through my pores.
Tell me
that you "Love" me,
make my heart feel anew.

Tell me,
just tell me!

Dreams (FOB Normandy—Iraq '08)

(2 Valerie)

I'm dreaming
of life at its perfection,
dreaming of love
with much adoration,
dreaming of beauty, and
a future beyond description.

I'm dreaming,
dreaming of you.

Brown Rose

(2 Valerie)

My eyes
have seen many roses,
My nose
has smelled many scented ones,
My fingers
have felt its many textures,
artificial and real,
My lips
have kissed many, but
if there be one so extraordinary, then surely you, for
My eyes
have yet to see
one like you,
My nose
has yet to smell
one scented like you,
My fingers
have yet to caress any like you, and
My lips
have yet to kiss one like you.

Sweet,
Beautiful,
Chocolate,
Fragranced, and
Smooth,

You're extraordinary,
Brown,
yet a Rose.

◇◇◇◇◇◇◇◇◇◇

I never really understood how soothing Roses were,
until the day I met you.

◇◇◇◇◇◇◇◇◇◇

I wanted to write about women in a different way. I
wanted to describe women in general as something
precious, but in a different tone. I asked myself what
could be more delicate and precious. So I thought of
a rose. Most women love roses, though for the longest
time I never understood why. But then I realized that
women are the fragile aspects of our macho lives. They
are as delicate as the roses we give them on birthdays,
anniversaries, etc., so I decided to write about them in
such a way in order for most guys to understand their
worth. I don't know of many guys who expect roses on
their birthdays or anniversaries rather than the new
Nikes, a car, etc. But as men we should cherish roses—
our women. We cuddle with them, smell them, miss
them, love them, so we should think of them as the
roses. Their aromas make us stand out as life's breeze
blows in our direction. This next poem is especially
dedicated to my Rose, and to all other roses that have
in some way touched my life and all other lives in
this world.

A Heartfelt Joy!

I'm healing
from scars of a hurtful past,
healing
from pain of broken hearts,
healing from the anger
beneath this smiling mask.

I'm falling,
falling in love with you!

◇◇◇◇◇◇◇◇◇◇

Though there are many things
of sweet taste and nature in our world,
if there be anything sweeter, more appeasing than these,
then it is spending quality time with you!

Anonymous

Hey.
Just wanted to say hi,
you're very beautiful, and
though they say
Angels come in disguise,
I know you're real,
a true sex appeal,
I can't explain
how you make me feel,
whether it be by
your looks,
your words,
your smile, or
Sexual/loving/sexing skills,
you are everything
I have never imagined,
ever wanted,
needed,
craved and
dreamt of!

"If you would be loved, love and be lovable."

Benjamin Franklin

Someone commented on this next poem and said,
"That's a pretty interesting thing to say about love." But
when you read the poem, you'll gather that most if not
all of what is written are true. Love comes on strong,

especially to an individual who has never experienced it before. It could lead you on with a string of promises in order to endow you with hope. And later, in the end, you're greeted with a shocking reality that love isn't what he/she said it is after all. Your heart is left in pieces. Your mind is dazed and confused, and you can't seem to figure out what went wrong. Everyone including me has had a similar experience whether we were the victim or victimizer.

When Love Says

(4 those who are fools 4 love)

When love says, "I love you,"
It makes you feel so good, but
Beware,
It's probably not so true.

When love says,
"You're very beautiful/handsome,"
It makes you feel so special, sophisticated, and
Confident within yourself, but
Beware,
It's probably just for the sex, and
Not wholly because of who you truly are.

When love says,
"You're my better half,
With thee, I shall stay forever,"
It enlightens your soul,
Makes you feel so wanted, but
Beware,
He/she probably won't always feel the same
When he/she finds the one
With whom he/she feels you can't compete.

When love says,
"You can count on me,
I'll always be there,"

You suddenly don't feel so alone,
It dispels your heart's despair, but
Beware,
He/she probably doesn't honestly care, and
Those same words will leave your heart to tear
When love says,
"I love you,"
Don't feel so alarmed,
Just hold him/her in your arms, and
With every sincerity in your heart,
Say, "I love you too,"
Only, if that's how you truly feel.

Just Laughing

I must tell you a story
Of a long ago mystery,
Of how my heart was entangled in misery
From a so sudden tragedy.

I used to be happy,
Smiling so much they called me smiley,
Until I met this girl name Cassey,
Who wanted us to get married

So off I went to the Army training course
To better our future of tomorrow,
But soon after, life spun outta control,
And few years later we were divorced!

I'm still very happy,
not so much smiling,
just laughing,
Can you imagine!

An Insidious Affair

(2 a flirt)

Dream
is what it seems,
sweeter than honey from the honeybees.
With pain
we share this Infatuation
deeper than most
whose True love flourishes to an end in vain.
And though in its twilight,
heartbroken is what we'd be,
we hopelessly strive
to turn this Lust of ours
into a loving reality!

I Want You Bad

Come 2 me lady,
give me all the passion you possess,
let me have it my way, because
I fantasize 'bout everything that's beneath your dress.
I want you, bad!

Come 2 me lady,
give me all the pleasures I've yet to have,
I can make it last all day,
I want you, bad!

Come 2 me lady,
let's enjoy the wonders of the skies,
you're the highlight of my days,
I'd love to watch the sunrise in between your thighs.

I want you, bad!

Apple Bottoms

Amazing
is what I call it,
firm hips,
bottoms round and big,
toned and bigger than my palms can fit.
It jiggles at every step
so smoothly as if breezing with the wind,
Damn!
Outta breath,
I can't even begin to express
the many sexual effects that I get
whenever you're around.

2 Minutes through Eternity

(One Night Stands)

I had fun 2night,
which makes it hard
to escape your sight,
I'd like 2 come in
just for a couple of minutes, or
2 sit 4 a while.
You are fun,
more than fun could ever be, and
in your eyes,
my future I see, for
if I made loving you my duty,
then it's evident that I shall never leave.
Kiss me, and
then in breathe,
U 2 shall believe what it is I see,
the wholeness of us,
makes reality a dream of peace.
There's no need
to be afraid, 'cause
I can sense the weakness in your knees,
let me make love 2 U, and
fulfill the fantasies of U and me, for,
after all this is done,
I promise to make it last
4 all eternity.

...2 days later, he hasn't called,
your pride succumbed to his game!

◇◇◇◇◇◇◇◇◇◇

Iraq was something, a whole new world, and for those that haven't been, it's not your average dream vacation. There are too many lonely nights, too many silent cries, and too many painful nightmares. And the whole time you're there, there's only one friend who remains loyal to you; that's loneliness. It wakes with you and falls asleep with you day in day out. It never fails.

But before April 7, 2007, when I was shipped off with an M249 machine gun and M4 to fight a war on terror, majority of the small things in life were taken for granted especially voices. You know how sometimes you get tired of hearing the other person talk over and over and over and again and how your phone be buzzing at two in the morning? Well, you don't share this luxury in Iraq. All you have to comfort you are the same things that scare you. The loud mortars, the sporadic gun fires and the ones lying on the cots next to you are the ones that love and annoy you. After a while, the voices you once got tired of hearing are the ones you treasure most and want to hear across the phone after waiting your turn in line for two hours or more. The poem that follows was written as I waited in line to call home August 24, 2007, when the vehicle I was driving got bombed with an EFP. You must know that it is by God's good grace and love that I'm still alive today.

When You Say Good-Bye

Voices are one of the many things in life
that we don't always seem to appreciate,
especially if it's not a radio tune
blasting the waves of our ears
just like ghetto music.
Softer than silk,
more relaxing than a sofa,
unlike most others,
your voice,
whether spoken aloud near
or whispered from afar,
gives me the true definition of sound,
and restores peace and harmony
to me in every state of mind, so
I dare not lose the magic of its Inspiration, because
it hurts me so badly
whenever you say Good-bye.

With You

some are fulfilled by worldly pleasures
for which they'd kill for,
fashion,
cars,
money,
some are fulfilled by Godly things
for which they'd die for,
the Bible,
heavens,
happy marriage,
salvation,
church teachings.
I possess worldly pleasures,
I love, enjoy and would die for Godly things, but
nothing is more fulfilling
than being with you.

◇◇◇◇◇◇◇◇◇◇

I went to Iraq knowing that I left home, family, and
friends who loved and completed me, but after I went
on my first few missions, the emptiness started to
occupy my heart. I felt alone and incomplete. It wasn't
just because I was away from friends and family, it was
due to something bigger than me. And if I were going
to stay alive, I needed to befriend somebody with more
fighting power than my machine guns and demolition.

I needed Jesus. So after I realized that, I wrote this poem, befriended Him, and took along with me Psalm 91 wherever I went.

Incomplete

I've got U
and two kids,
wonderful as wonder could be, but
sometimes I feel as though
I'm still the single me,
wandering this earth,
trying to find mind peace,
a quiet place 4 my head to sleep, and
treasured memories to keep.

Haunted
by the past behind me,
afraid to meet the future be4 me,
I lack a vital piece of me
that makes a man complete,
a piece that thou cannot give me, and
it's a He,
Jesus!

Incomplete II

I have a heart
full of love, but
a life with no Romance, so
every night I dream,
hoping 2 find the one
who'd move me forward, and
rid my life of this unwanted suspense.

Selfless

I've sacrificed my heart
once again for its desires of wholesomeness,
crippling my feelers from the start,
for Ur love to drown me in her weakness
just to fulfill your fantasies, and
all that Ur body aspires.

If I Love U

If I love you,
there'd be no need
to wonder if I do.
If I love you,
there'd be no reason
not to trust you.
If I love you,
there'd be no need
to find yourself a better me.
If I love you,
there'd be no reason
to frighten yourself
at the sound of my name.
If I love you,
there'd be no reason
to sit in solitude and cry.
If I love you,
there'd be no reason
for you to ask yourself why, because
If I love you,
there'd be no need
to wonder if I do.

I Do

I know
that I sometimes
tend to behave unfair, but
if encase you were wondering
as to whether
I love you,
need you,
want you,
trust you,
crave you,
think of you,
dream of you,

I do!

If I Think of You

If I think of you,
in pain, I will cry,
outpouring bodies of water from my eyes, because
it hurts me that we didn't try, only
if I think of you.

If I think of you,
I will remember the undying truth
of the innocent love we shared as youths, because
it makes it hard to forget
all of the lies you once told, only
if I think of you.

If I think of you,
in hopelessness I will falter,
to speak of Us and our failed love to others, because
loneliness taunts and haunts me, only
if I think of you.

No, Not You!

My love,
when I say You,
I speak of Us,
not as two, but
the one whole
that really means nothing to You!

Alone

I'm alone,
Alone in this world of many homes.
I'm alone,
Alone on mystery's throne.

I'm alone,
Alone in my thoughts.
I'm alone,
Alone when we're on the phone,
I'm alone,
Even when you're seated next to me at home.

I'm alone,
Alone whether near or afar.
I'm alone,
Alone when we make love beneath the stars.

I'm alone,
Alone in my dreams.
I'm alone,
Even if you're the blood that flows through my veins.

I'm alone,
Alone
All alone!

Abed

Where bodies rumble,
your legs astride me
in passions bundled.

Where sheets sweat,
the meet of your thighs,
tingles in juices so warm and wet.

Where love unfolds,
the truth and lies of our hearts,
in secrets are told!

With Me, Tonight

With me,
let thee stay tonight,
Your absence
overwhelms my heart with fright,
With me,
let thee try tonight,
to save our love from her twilight.
With me,
let thee dream beautiful dreams of tomorrow tonight,
to enjoy fairytales and forget our fuss and fights.
With me,
let thee lay and make love tonight,
until our bodies climax.
With me,
let thee cry tonight,
for all of our plights.
With me,
let thee talk tonight,
and rid this unbearable silence from our lives.
With me,
let thee breathe tonight
and enjoy the pleasantness of nature's breeze.
With me,
let thee unconditionally Love tonight
as though there's no tomorrow, because
unto us, tomorrow isn't Promised!

Appreciated Appreciation

I rumbled in my life
with solitude and fear,
hoping to find someone true who'd care
and help me rid memories
of all the losses and pain that
my heart has had to bear, but
the world stayed cold,
with no one to hold,
no confidant to confide in
until you walked in the door.

Your love has delivered me,
happiness has found me,
peace lives in me, and
from all the evil of this world,
I've been freed,
You're my appreciated appreciation, and
I love U.

I was once confused,
hope was hopeless to me,
the future seemed bright, but
darkness corrupted my sight, blinding me,
love seemed so surreal,
heartbreaks, betrayals, and deceits
were my life's ordeals,
in all the earth,

I couldn't find 4 me,
a real love and sex appeal
until you walked in the door.

Your love has delivered me,
happiness has found me,
peace lives in me, and
for all the evil of this world,
I've been freed,
you're my appreciated appreciation,
I love U.

Loved 2 Love Her

(4 my ride and die hood chicks)

Mama
says she's no good,
when they first spoke,
she didn't like her tone or her mood.
Her dress code
isn't very homey,
her speech isn't spoken to standard.
Papa
says to me, "You're a grown man," and
no more a child.
I see that she makes you smile, but
I don't think she's worth your while,
so just wait to find a better one in time."
Family
tends to feel the same way, because
2 them, this is all she is, but
still,
I'd Loved 2 Love Her!

How Should I Live

Since you've been gone,
I've become paralyzed, because
now I realize
that you are the working part
of this body in which I dwell.
So tell me,
how should I live without you
when you're my life's motive,
the only reason 4 which I breathe.
Since you disappeared,
I live with loneliness in fear, because
it's only me who cares
about the falling tears and pain I bear.
So tell me,
how should I live without you
when you're the function of my heart,
the only one
keeping me from falling apart?

How should I live?

Shall We Dance

We've spent
most of our times
living in pretense,
smiling,
when we meant to cry,
happy,
when times were sad, but,
baby,
I'd like you understand,
that loving U
is all that has ever made sense
in this world
where there's no evidence
of love's existence
amongst men, but
now as the music plays,
sweeping our minds away, and
our bodies lost in Romance,
Shall we dance?

Repeat

I know that you've heard
all this before, but
I'd still like to say that
you are everything
heavenly to me,
your love completes me,
your life fulfills mine,
your persona
is one of a kind; indefinable
and indescribable,
loving you every day,
4 me, is like living in repeat, so
this is my love in repeat.

I LOVE U

Revolutionary Love

I need love,
one that's blind and
sees no flaws,
I need love,
one that's tender and
gentle without cause.
I need love,
one that talks and
is always willing to listen.
I need love,
one that'll cry
with me, even
if she knows not why.
I need love,
one that sounds like music
but doesn't scold nor gossip.
I need love,
one that shines like the sun, and
is willing to sometimes dim like the moon.
I need love,
one that dreams, but
isn't afraid to live in reality.
I need love,
one that's a fairytale, but
isn't a fictional tale.
I need love,
one that's revolutionary.

I need love,
one with flexibility and versatility.
I need love,
True Love.

2 Pieces

I exist in 2 pieces,
Trying to find a way
To make me whole,
Encrusting in this metallic body,
A fragile heart
That has one too many times
Been torn apart, and
The distance between us
Brings me so much fear, because
The peace of my mind
dwells well within your soul.

My Betta Half

While U were gone,
I found me,
lost in stress and pain,
I discovered me,
hoping in hopelessness,
loving through a vague heart,
praying that time would keep us apart,
by nightmares,
I had been chastised, but
then I understood why,
it is Us that my heart despises.
While U were out,
I knew that I wanted me again,
not the old me, because
that'd mean that I'd have to be with you,
the new me that
I discovered, found and saw, but
then I dreamed of you,
crying on bended knees,
praying that time
would bring me back to U,
to shine through the darkness of Ur life, so
that U too can find, discover and see U, because
it is I that bring the best outta U,

it is I that complete U, so
now I've realized that
You and I were meant to be, because
U are everything that I'm not.
U are my better half.

He Says, She Says (Lovers' Blues)

He says,
"U make beauty
hard to define, but
if it were the only word
in the dictionary,
I'd use Ur name to define it."

So She says,
"You're a charmer,
very sweet indeed,
you make my frozen spirit glow, and
make my hidden feelings show,
thank you."

He says,
"Anytime,
I can't help but
say how I feel; the truth,
you're the oxygen
in the air I breathe,
the only known reason
for which I exist."

So She says,
"You make
a broken heart love again,
with you,

love feels like a surprise,
the unknown feeling I feel,
so pleasant and sweet,
that warms up my soul
only when you speak.
I love you."

He says,
"You're the crown on my head, because
with you,
I'm King,
Your love teaches me
to perfect my speech,
the sweet words I speak,
is inspired by you, because
with you,
my soul has its Peace.
I love you 2!"

Untitled

I don't wanna fail at this,
if this is what must be, 'cuz
I promise to love you so hard
until I make Ur blinded eyes see.
Your heart is fragile 2 me,
full of sweet emotions and pain,
afraid to fall in love, so
from my love you tend to flee.
You are very true indeed,
your persona is that of a queen, so
I don't wanna fail at this
if this is what must be, because
loving you sets me free.

Hello, Do You Hear Me?

Hello,
do you hear my voice
speaking to thee,
a speech of love and peace?
You've hardened your heart, and
though we may be One
I don't feel the wholeness of Us, because
We live as two, and
I'm no longer able
to play my part in loving
and reaching out to U.

Hello,
do you hear me?

Beyond the End of Time

You awaken to the crow of a chicken,
loud noises,
an alarm clock,
stretching like a gladiola,
smiling gently, because
I lay next to you.

You fight sleep when darkness falls,
throwing tantrums like a baby,
frowning at the easy pace of time,
you are afraid that by morning,
this life would neither be yours nor mine.

Even though
I possess a different mind, body, and soul,
I love you equally, and
this makes us one whole.

I'd pace myself to your heartbeat,
if I could,
moving slower than a snail or turtle, because
I don't wanna miss the joy
of every second spent with you.

So when everything perishes, and
all of this life passes onto the next,
you'll always be a living part of me, thus,

no matter life or no life,
I'll love you truly,
today and forever,
beyond the end of time.

Sex (None Like Mine)

Amazed,
her eyes are fixed upon me,
mind flustered, yet in a haze,
it's clear that
she has never once before felt this way,
so she says,
"wonderful isn't a word to describe It,
truth isn't a word to call It,
extraordinary doesn't honestly explain It,
there's been nothing like this for me before you,
to possess my body,
cherishing all of its components,
fulfilling all that it desires,
allowing my soul and emotions to aspire,
hmm,
let's do It again and again and again
till our bodies tire,
let's do It again and again and again
till the deeds of darkness transpire,
give it to me,
deep, deep, and deeper, 'cuz
baby you're truly a keeper,
give it to me,
deep, deep, and deeper, 'cuz
you make me an honest feeler,
give it to me,
deep, deep, and deeper 'cuz

baby it tastes like a reefer,
do it to me,
till I become breathless,
do it to me,
I wanna feel restless,
hmm, give it to me, SEX.

Haiku

Honesty is one of man and woman's great virtues, but
it's only after we lie,
when lies we begin to speak.

Cheater (Song)

I hate that look in your eyes, because
baby I know all that follows are lies,
it was only before
that your words had me hypnotized, but
since you stepped outside of Us,
I've realized that loving you isn't worth my while,
and it's unfortunate that you and I
have brought into this world an innocent child
'cuz you're cheater.

Stop right there,
just close the door and say no more.
It's time to stop playing your silly games, and
though it's hard 4 me to say this,
I don't love you anymore,
cheater, cheater, cheater.

I remember it like yesterday,
when the picture perfect you walked my way,
beautiful and genuine as beauty can be,
lighting up the darkness in me,
not thinking that one day it'd turn out to be
everything that my heart isn't willing to keep
making it hard for my lungs to breathe,
'cause you're a cheater.

Stop right there,
just close the door and say no more,
It's time to stop playing your silly games, and
though it's hard 4 me to say this
I don't love you anymore!

Come Back 2 Me (Song)

Since you left,
I've become everything but me,
doing everything from fornicating
to clubbing and throwing up in the bathroom sink,
trying to find sanity,
your love gave my life a meaningful meaning, and
now in your absence,
I live life teetering on the edge of insanity.

Baby please come back 2 me,
I know I can't do everything, but
I'm willing to do anything
to make U and I a better We.

Baby,
I know I've told many lies,
that dispelled the beauty of us from your eyes, but
it's only you that I adore, and
it hurts now that you and I are no more, so

Baby, please come back 2 me,
I know I can't do everything, but
I'm willing to do anything
to make U and I a better We.

Feud

So I looked at myself,
said to myself,
there can't be peace with anyone else,
not with you, her, the one before and after you, but
just myself.

So she looked at herself,
said to herself,
there can't be true love with anyone else,
not you, him, the one before or after you, but
just myself.

Applaud Me

I'm
not just another nigga
focused on his chedda',
I'm
not the beast you label me,
a drunkard or cheater, because
I'm
the only one who knows Ur worth,
the only one who loves U,
takes care of U,
no matter the constraints, so
instead of berating and belittling me,
Woman,
Applaud Me!

If

If I said,
"I love U,"
would U say
U love me 2?
If I said.
"I want U,"
would U invite
me into U?
If I said,
"You are beautiful,"
would U say that
I'm handsome 2?
If I choose to care 4 U,
would U care 4 me 2? And
though I feel all the above
about and for you,
don't answer these questions
if your words will not be true!

Mystery Girl

I've seen her
thousands of times,
made love to her a million times,
spoken of her every time
she crossed my mind,
which is all the time.

I've yet to meet her,
I don't know what to say to her,
she's more than just diamonds and pearls,
nothing like ordinary girls,
her dreams, compared to theirs,
aren't the same,
everything about her
is insanely sane.

I don't know her.
She lives somewhere in my dreams,
but she touches me like reality,
her silence keeps me company,
she's everything I cannot understand, but
she's everything that my heart demands,
she roams the dreams of every man, but

none of them can notice her
nor see her like I can, and
being with her till the End
is my life's master plan.

Who is my mystery girl,
are you my mystery girl?

Beauty

(4 Nature)

Once,
Beauty was beautiful,
Born,
innocent into this world
in its Genesis, but
only after a few days,
she met her demise
at the hands of men.

Why must thee
call Urself beautiful
when beauty exists
not in or amongst us?
The world
is blind to beauty, for
our eyes have seen evil,
our hearts are full of
hate and iniquity.

Once
Beauty was beautiful, but
Ever since she met men,
Beauty was beautiful no more!

Tears

Oh, Tears,
why must thou fall upon me,
relieving me of this pain I feel,
when heartbreak numbs my heart
depleting its feelings?

Oh, Tears,
why must thou wash me free
from this feeling of captivity
when this evil world
still holds me captive,
vulnerable to pain?

Oh, Tears
Oh, Tears...

Sweetest Taboo

(4 da queens @ clubs)

I've heard
that loving eyes are blind, and
sometimes it's hard
4 a man to speak the truth, but
you, and I cannot be true.

You're everything I am,
sweet, tender, loving, & caring, but
you're everything I dare not be,
lustful, deceitful, and promiscuous, and
though my heart seeks the world 4 u,
with every weakness of my spirit
I must resist you, because
you're just the sweetest taboo.

You're thought of
more than my most desired fantasies,
sex with you,
is just another dream of mine revealed,
your touch caresses and bestows warmth.
Saying your name to friends
feels as though I live in fame, because
you're everything they want,
a freak, sexy, speaking the perfect body language, but
you're everything my life won't keep, and
though my heart feels complete with you,

with every desires of my body and soul,
I must resist you, because
you're just my sweetest taboo.

06/19/07

(so I married my friend)

A new chapter began
with little words
written or said,
"I do."
Happiness
became my friend,
with hope
that this joy never ends,
4 better 4 worse,
till death do us part.

Cupid (A Letter to You)

(4 my Heart's Hate 4 Love)

I bear a hardened heart,
sheltered in a burning flesh,
this unwanted feeling
makes me feel as though
my mind dwells in a mesh,
locked away from sanity,
overwhelmed by paranoia, because
love hasn't been kind to me.

Sometimes
I wanna be dissected, but
there are no analytical reasons
for me to feel this way,
if love is truly love.

Sometimes
I wanna cry, but
when tears fall,
it gives me no reasons to love
if love be pain.

Cupid,
Oh Roman god of love,
teach me to love,
soften my soul
so that in my heart's

hate for love
I will grow older, and
love her again.
Help me love her again!

To Be with U

To be with U is a chance
for which my heart earnestly seeks,
to live in romance
of which my words are unable to speak.
U live healthily
with a bleeding heart,
fighting to heal from your life's hurtful past, and
though I'm no angel, I'm still a man
endeavoring to make U happy
as though it were my command, but
all I ask is for one chance
to rid U of all the miseries that life has put U through,
for
at the end of the day,
you'll realize that I'm nothing but true, because
this lonely heart of mine belongs to U.

Heat

Hormones,
    spell binding,
    my body lies twitching,
    with warmth, my skin itches,
Let's lay naked, fulfilling love in the Everglades.

Emotions,
    blindingly sought,
    I feel of passion's touch,
    so personal, powerful, soft and yet rough,
Spread your hips, kiss my lips, and
with Sex in lust, entice my soul!

Adultery

Somewhere in another room,
you lay nude in another man's arms, and
though he's not your groom,
U R still seduced by his charm.
So sometimes when I'm alone,
I often ponder
why a man and woman must say, "I do"
when infidelity shadows their minds,
as they walk closely hand in hand,
leading one another down lost paths,
that True love shall never find?
Why must a Man and Woman
in the presence of God
share matrimonial vows,
when to love faithfully,
they know not how?

Why?
That I've yet to fully understand.

Churching Me (Hypocrisy)

I don't wanna go to hell,
can't you tell
by the way I carry myself?
Nicely groomed, smelling of Curve,
handsomely tailored.
I don't wanna go to hell.

I don't wanna burn in everlasting fire,
can't you see I'm no liar
by the way I speak my tongue?
Clean speech, singing Gospel songs,
stomping my feet in my church choir,
I don't wanna burn in everlasting fire.

I don't wanna die in sin,
can you see I'm not like him?
Pussyfooting after Women,
drowning myself in bottles,
I don't wanna die in sin.

I don't wanna go to hell,
can't you tell
by the way I carry myself?

Macho in my steps,
not pursing my lips, or
winking my eyes,
I don't wanna go to hell, but
my mistress on my cell.

I don't wanna go to hell!

When Men Talk

I belong to a gender
of which most people talk, but
it's nothing compared
to the words spoken
when men talk.
Shawty got back,
pursing our lips,
I'd hit that in back of my Cadillac.
Nigga,
her face ain't all that, but
s——t she got a body, and
I know it feels good in between dem thighs.
Damn,
look at dem DSLs,
I heard that she give good head, and
I don't care
if the bitch is all 'bout my bread.
Hey, bro,
would U hit that?
Na, nigga, I'm married.
S——t, that don't mean s——t,
I am too, but
I'll beat the bricks off that
Hispanic, black, African, Asian, or white pussy.
Sad it is, but
only few mention God,
Home, Family, and things that matter, but

Money, Cars, Promiscuity, and Hoes
are the most things spoken of
when men talk!

A Kiss of Night (Infidelity)

Softly
felt all over the body,
in every component of the soul,
her tongue melts like jelly,
so possessive,
yet in a genuine manner,
hands clinching her belly,
ignoring his wife on the celly.
Brain frozen,
colder than ice,
temperature still rising,
trapped in a sexual escapade,
the thought of having moral responsibilities, and
living up to his vows
is now an immoral surprise.

Maybe Love Fears Me

Sometimes I sit
and watch the many passersby go by,
with love written so lovely in their eyes,
lips touching,
arms hugging,
hands caressing,
fingers pleasing, and
then I begin to wonder why
must loneliness be one with me,
why must sadness seize my heart,
why must heartbreaks continuously make me cry? And
then it dawns to me that
I possess a tender spirit
where true love resides,
where commitment and honesty are merits, and
though to each other
the rest of the world is so Untrue,
living Love as a lie,
I still remain Real, so
Maybe Love fears me!

The Bachelor

Ever since she passed,
He hadn't had the courage to approach another soul,
especially now grayed, and few centuries old,
in his head are many bedtime stories, but
he has no kids, so they can't be told.

Everyone's lips have something to say,
wondering how he lives in such a dismay,
how he still smiles in a humble way, but
in his head, he knows that
it's always a Joyful blessing to breathe through another
a day.

Miss Betty Bee

She arose to the stand
shining brighter than the summer day,
hoping now that she'd take his hands
so that together, forever they'd stay.

Fate was everything she never understood, because
fairytales of eternal romance kept her so blind
from noticing all the evil that he could do,
especially when with his friends, he'd spend more time.

And now that she's swollen up front,
he hides behind the drugs and bottles,
insensitive to her needs or wants,
leaving her alone to carry on through her tedious
struggles.

I'll never do this again, she now says to herself
staring at their seed, and
the many dusty wedding photos seated up on her shelf,
and
though he leaves her nightly to cheat with Miss
Supermodel Mary Jane,
Jane could never possess the beautiful and strong
womanly characteristics
as her, Lonely Miss Betty Bee!

Mr. Insecure

He spends his life
fighting to please her own,
doing all that she asks,
burying his hurting heart as though in a tomb.
I don't mind, is an excuse he'd make
holding back his tears,
while hoping not to cross her in any way,
as if for him, she honestly cared.
Beautiful outwardly is all she ever was, because
he felt so proud if whilst together, someone else saw.
In his head,
he knew he wanted to escape this nightmare, but
her love, he faithfully tried to procure, because
with or without it, he'd always be Mr. Insecure.

Shattered Dreams

Together as 1,
you spirit my gloomy days,
edifying my hopeless ways.
You and I
could never be 2, because
nothing right is done without you, and
whenever I am alone,
every word of my lips
express my emptiness and desires of you.
With you,
I don't have to work hard
for a better future, because
I'm able to see
how beautiful and complete it is
whenever I look at you.
Baby,
my future is you, but
now as I lay here
trying to dream 'bout you,
it isn't you alone that I see.
I see someone who is not a he
replacing me!

Ecstasy

Last night we lay naked
locked in a sexual embrace,
speaking so softly
of love in many different languages,
enjoying fairytales we thought eternal.
The air between us
was warm yet brisk,
so fulfilling and peaceful.
Once again,
I had placed my heart at risk
of loving, love making and heartbreak, because
I knew that when I awoken,
You'd be gone,
gone with another,
as fast as the wind.

Is This the Way Love Goes?

Sleepless nights;
Long, empty days;
countless fuss and fights;
despondency,
teary eyes,
vague smiles,
unhappiness,
is this the way love goes?

Unfading lies,
meaningless thoughts,
berating words,
physical and mental abuse,
desertion,
no appreciation,
undutiful,
promiscuity,
unfaithfulness,
is this the way love goes?

Is this the way love goes?
I'd like to know, because
I would rather die in solitude
than for love to leave
my heart and soul destitute!

A Bad Chick (ALERT)

I call her a Georgia Peach,
she needs no light,
her beauty shines past the sun,
she turns the heads of men,
even missionaries,
her presence is just a mystery,
she's every girl's Barbie,
every woman's wanna be,
every boy's dream,
every man's most-wanted queen,
everyone she has ever loved
sustained a heart injury, because
when she would leave,
their hearts would irregularly beat,
their lungs had no air to breathe, and
for this,
she lived with pride and conceit,
shutting out every common man sincere to her
or wealthier than a king, but
just when she thought she'd found Mr. Right,
life shut out her lights, because
along with him came his son,
Jerry HIV.

Emotions of Yesterday, Today, Tomorrow

(2 those who were, are, and will be part of my life)

Yesterday,
There were many Roses,
who bloomed beautifully
in every color,
each of whom showed me
everything wonderful 'bout life,
whether or not in times of gloom.
But as the sun rose
to show me the heated side
of our cool dreams, fairytales and delusions,
all of my said Roses
soon withered, because
my love became incapable
of keeping them alive.

Today,
There are now many Roses,
each of whom blooms beautifully
in every color,
each of whom shows me
something new 'bout life each day
whether or not in times of gloom.
And even as the sun Rises
to broaden the heated side

of our shared cool fantasies,
delusions, dreams and fairytales,
all of said Roses still blossom, because
my love is capable of keeping them alive.

Tomorrow,
There will be many more Roses,
each of whom I hope will bloom beautifully
to show and teach me
all there is to life,
whether or not in times of gloom.
And if the sun does rise
to invade whatever
cool fairytales, delusion, fantasies and dreams,
we may share,
I hope that
all of said Roses
will indeed blossom by my side
whether or not,
my love is capable of keeping them alive!

A Mirage

U and Me
happily ever after,
is what I see
though our love is a total disaster.

A Probability

U and Me,
happy together as one
in reality,
despite the fact that our feelings
4 each other
are long gone!

How Can I Not Love Her

I
was once lonely,
running through life blindly, but
She
took me in
lovingly as one of hers,
as though I were her next of kin.

Rewind

Remember when we vowed to love
Each other unconditionally
Whether
In sickness or in health, for better for worst,
No matter the circumstances of life, until
Death do us part?

I still do.

Lonely

There are two of us,
three of us,
so many of us, but
I can't see any of you
except a glimpse of
unknown shadows.
There are tears,
fear, anger, pain, love,
along with two of us,
three of us,
so many of us, but
I can't feel anyone
calming me,
urging me to say
what/how I feel.
There's yesterday,
today, tomorrow,
along with two of us,
three of us,
so many of us, but
I can't see any of you
in my past,
my present or future.
Why go on
when there are two of us,

three of us,
so many of us, and
none of us,
including you
cares about me?

Take Me Away

I don't control my own destiny,
this I know, but
I don't wanna suffer through eternity, so
now that my life is a wreck,
take me away.

It is said that there are brighter days,
this I know, but
I don't wanna keep dying inside, hoping to live
through a happy day that's not promised unto me, so
now that my life is just a shadow,
take me away.

The downfall of men is not the end of life,
this I know, but
it's hard to go on daily through a life full of strife, so
now that I see no future for me,
take me away.

It is said that love without madness is no love,
this I know, but
if madness is what our love entails,
I hope love will never know to say my name, and
now that I can finally let go,
Take me away!

Haven

Vibrant,
quiet, peaceful, warming.
In solitude,
it is my fortitude.
So, homey,
my only appetence,
gosh,
I love it here
in your arms!

Life Support

Most people
run through life
without knowing
what keeps them alive.
They wander, they lurk
until death steals them by surprise.
But ever since your love
came and took my heart away,
I've enjoyed watching the sunrise
whether it's through the skies,
your eyes, your smiles or
in between your thighs, because
I've learned the importance of life, and
it means more than just living
to me now than it has ever before.
You keep me alive,
whether it's by your love,
your tears,
your touch,
your words,
even when you're mad.
So if your heart should fail, or
your love stops,
my life ends.
I'm one with you,
nothing but lifeless without you.
You are my life,
my life support.

My Woman

She
defines my character,
nurtures my dying soul,
warms my frozen spirit,
lightens my dark ways,
She completes me.

She's
the air I breathe,
the words I speak,
the thoughts I think,
the blood I bleed,
the beautiful sight I see,
She lives in me.

She
teaches me
the importance of life,
thinks like knowledge,
strives for success,
lives for the best,
She inspires me!

Gold of My Heart, Pearl of the Sea

(2 a Crush)

She is only One
valuing a value of a thousand or Two
In my heart,
she is mine alone, but
in reality she belongs to me and a Few

I could hold her all night
tirelessly scrambling for the treasure between her
THIGHS.
She would oblige me the pleasure, but
she is another man's priceless treasure.

I'd cry whenever she had to leave, because
she took away the only scented air I could breathe.
But still she couldn't understand why she meant this
much to me,
even though I called her the gold of my heart,
when she was just a peal of the sea.

I've Changed

If only U
could see beyond our past,
U would believe me
when I say how beautiful U are.

Woman,
not all of what I say are lies,
even though sometimes Ur questions
come most shocking than a surprise,
I still want U 2 be a part of my imperfect life.

It's not pleasant 2 say, "I love U," and
then watch U leave, but
if that's what a lonely reality means,
then I'll do all I can to be with U
because I desire not to be alone.

U love me,
I love U 2, so
don't overshadow our emotions
by my little wrong doings, because
U as a Woman, Lover, and Best Friend,
mean more than these words, and
the entirety of the world 2 me.

All Night Long

Let me sing 4 U a song
that rhymes with rhythms of our motional bodies,
softly in ur ears
leaving ur eyes to tear.

It's a song
I wrote many years ago
when puberty came along, and
now as I play with features of ur naked body,
those written words will make ur temperature soar.

Lord knows
how long I've waited for this day, so
let's make and taste juices,
let's whisper and scream emotions,
let's move and groove to our heartbeats,
let's lay, sit, or stand on our feet,
let's love and make love in any manner we please,
all night long!

Private Letter

Girl,
I've watched you mope 'round town,
head bowed from street to street.
Your walls of emotions have tumbled down, so
your heart and soul abide in a bundle of grief.

Woman,
All men are not the same,
spreading juices from hole to hole,
trying to stay at best at his game,
degrading lilies and roses,
especially the ones who flourishes wildly around strip
poles.

Beautiful,
give me the opportunity
to turn your life around for the best, and
no matter life at its worst,
it is my promise that
your worth will always be a known reality.

So Angel,
as the seconds, minutes, hours & days pass on by, and
our hearts war with loneliness,
our bodies age,

give me the opportunity
to bring you beautiful smiling years, because
I so much hate to see you cry!

Yours Truly

Trust Me

Yes,
there will be answers
for every question that you may ask,
sincere and true,
some of which you may not want to hear.
there will be reasons
for every action and reaction,
fair and impartial,
some of which you may not want to bear, but
none of said answers, actions or reactions
will give you a reason to doubt
that I love you truly, so
just give me your heart, and
trust me.

Part 2

But the Past Shall Remain the Past!

Fiction

Once upon a time,
I made me believe
that time would never
let you leave,
I fell in love with U,
believing that one day,
U 2 will love me, but
Once upon a time,
it was just a dream, because
we turned out to be untrue, and
time proved to me that
U were never mine!

E. L. Ellis

(2 Emma)

When U first complimented me,
I knew U and I would be.
Your long dark hair,
caramel skin,
firm curves,
beautiful smiles,
were everything wonderful
that my eyes had ever seen.
I finally believed that
love had come 2 rescue me
from solitude and dire, and
2 share with me my fantasies.
Your long late night conversations
after work,
listening 2 music 2gether
from across the phone,
made me believe that
the lost part of me
had finally found its way home.
The sound of Ur name
elated the depressed spirit in me.
Like you,
I was shadowed by fear, but
I knew that I'd be dumb
if for you, I choose not to care, so
we kissed and made love

in the darkness of the beach
against the fast February wind
brushing up against our bodies
as we held onto each other tightly, but
after we let go,
sex, friends, and money
took away whatever happiness
that came to be, and
ever since then,
I've come to realized
that all we shared
were series of broken dreams,
dreams that I've yet to awaken from
dreams that U and him now share in reality.

Old Road's Love (Liberia 2001)

(2 Stephenette D. Snoh)

everyone was someone's friend,
everyone was everyone's lookout,
everyone was everyone's messenger, and
now, just thinking of you, I remember,
writing and receiving scented letters,
sitting on my front porch
waiting to see you pass,
saying to myself, I gotta make this last.

parents weren't the greatest approving authority,
youngsters like us,
couldn't feel what we felt at such a teen age,
sneaking with you at night
only forced their hearts to rage, and
now, just thinking of you, I remember
getting yelled at for being in love with you,
rubbing your scars
after getting beat on for hours, because
you wouldn't let go of me,
saying to yourself, This is real as real can be.

friends soon became jealous,
they couldn't have what we had,
telling lies to see you and I fall, but
you and I held each other closer through it all, and
now, just thinking of you, I remember,

picking you up at school
just to be seeing together,
sneaking in the back room to make love,
vowing with the Bible and blood,
to always stay in love,
yesterday, today, and tomorrow, and
now, just thinking of it, I remember
how much we cried when we had to say good-bye.

And now as I write about it,
just thinking of you, I remember
how much I haven't forgotten about you!

Unmask Me

(2 Nisey)

Unfold me
Into the broken pieces I am, and
Let me rot to the unfading memories of you,
For at the end of the day,
I'll be just another man
Whom your heart failed to understand.

It felt like summer in July
On this beautiful cold winter night,
When I embedded my face
In the utopia between the meat of your thighs, and
For that moment,
It seemed as though life escaped me
When I breathed its sweet scent and
Became high.

For so long,
I've raged my heart with hate,
Letting go something so good
That I thought would've been a waste, but
Just remembering its sweet pleasant taste,
I fantasize of a special day
When with thee, I shall lay to copulate.

Unhide me
From beneath these tears, and

Let me express my pain and fears,
For at the end of all this,
I'll prove that my love wasn't a true lie,
A deceit nor a snare, because
You're a Woman for whom, I wanted to Care.

I Hate U

(2 da adulteress)

Loved you unconditionally, but
I was unappreciated,
so unhappy,
you decocted my life,
cheated on me as though
it were okay,
screaming his name
during sex,
impregnated by him,
claiming it was mine,
you're a swine, and
I hate U.

Cassandra

(2 my ex)

There was a time
when You and I
shared the same thoughts,
possessing one mind.
There was a time
when we shared
the same dreams,
possessing one future,
whether different or the same.

But
there came a time,
when 2gether
we could no longer be seen, because
we became individuals, and
no longer a team.
I'm sorry,
to have caused you so much pain,
shattering our lives
into series of broken dreams,
despite our efforts
2 stay one in the same.
I know you're happy with someone
who treats U better than a queen, and

I'm happy 4 U
even if for me,
Your heart doesn't feel the same.

Good-Bye

Sorry
that it has to end, but
our life together
is so difficult to comprehend,
love and trust,
our hearts have failed to implement, and
though in our eyes,
we seem so content,
being with you
overwhelms my soul with contempt.

Darling, even though
this isn't much of a compliment,
I know that you know
you deserve better, and
I don't want us
to hold on any longer, so
let's just wipe away our tears
and say, "Good-bye!"

"Goodbye!"

You, Aries

(2 the Aries that broke my heart)

I've struggled
To understand all the facts
Which have turned out
To be all real lies,
Telling me you loved me,
Knowing I was right there
In between your thighs.

You say the sweetest of things
That in my mind
makes me feel like a king.
You say the meanest of things
That makes my uplifted spirit sink.

Your words,
So appeasing, soothing, sexual, and sweet
Can make the hardest of hearts meek, but
Your touch,
So gentle, tender, and soft,
Makes my skin creep,
Cutting the inside of me,
leaving my soul to bleed.

In my mind,
You're most beautiful than beauty,
The only queen I see, but

In my eyes,
You're uglier than she. Ugly,
the devil who roams my nightmares.

In my dreams,
I can't live without you.
In my fantasies,
I don't wanna live without you, but
In reality,
I'm way better off without you!

02/04/05

(4 Cassie and I)

2 years ago from today,
I didn't think this day
would be a reality,
I dreamed,
hoped,
prayed, and
now U stand next to me
vowing to stay
for all eternity,
4 betta, 4 worse,
2 make babies and
build a happy family.
Thank You!

03/16/07

(2 Cassie and me; the split)

4 years ago,
this day wasn't thought of,
talked about,
dreamt of, because
happiness was what
we shared,
love was something for
which we cared, but
now cries and good-byes,
are the only things
left for us to hear.
I would've never imagined
that we'd leave
each other's heart and eyes
2 tear, but
I guess this is an inevitable pain
that we have to bare, so
4 what it's worth,
I'm sorry that U and I
can no longer be a pair.

Untitled

(4 those curious)

Today I thought:
there were 5 years,
2 years of love,
1 year of engagement,
2 years of marriage,
9 months of which
was a painful separation,
then harshly came the divorce,
all in a flash
just like a rash, but
tomorrow,
I shall be cured and
will remember this no more.

Anytime

(2 Stephenette D. Snoh)

The stars
remind me of how
we glowed beautifully in the dark.
The sun
reminds me of how bright
we shone together, even in the light.
The sun and moon
remind me of how
vital we were to each other.
Music reminds me
of how your voice
Took me to ecstasy.
Does anything remind
you of me?
Do you think about us
anytime?

Friends and Foes

(White teeth, black heart)

Sometimes
when life becomes so unjust, and
there's no one left to trust,
in my heart,
I have no friends, because
in my eyes,
all I see are foes!

Remembrance

(2 all in my past)

In memory of you,
I've held onto certain thoughts
that I thought vital to me.
I've held onto certain dreams
that I thought would make your absence
seem somewhat sane.
I remember your sex,
the mellowness of your voice
even when you screamed my name.
I remember your touch,
how you squeezed me gently
just right when you came.
I remember your kiss
possessing my lips
while my hands caress your hips
making its way down around your thighs
and in between where it splits.
I remember your tear drops
smeared over beautiful love letters
scented with your perfume
that you wrote to me.
I've held onto you,
though not physically so, but
this wholeness of me
means nothing if I let you go.
In memory of you,

I remember me
on bended knees praying
for U to come and rescue me
from my captor; loneliness.
Then U found another happiness,
left me in sadness, but
still I remember You, and
I'd just like to know
if you remember me too.

Epiphany

(2 da girl on 108th Street)

Breezing through life,
numbed of all things painful or loving,
Miss Lover Heartbreaker befriended my lost soul
fulfilling it with pleasure, lust, and greed.
She spoke as if from a different breed,
her words came across my ears like a creed
so tasteful and seductive like a sip of mead.
Her lips kissing on me,
wetly riding up and down my cone,
made me feel high on speed, but
kept my insipid heart in tone.
I wouldn't call it a fairytale,
neither would I call it a dream, but
a short lived fantasy, because
I soon came to see
that she was every guy's singing towhee,
humming hypnotizing melodies of different genres,
blowing away their brains, and
doing to them
all that she had done to me.

My Breakup Letter

Dear, Baby,
just for a second today,
I stopped and looked at our lives,
counted our fights;
One thousand ninety six painful days, and
One thousand ninety five miserable nights,
that's three long years,
of nothing but unhappy tears.
Whilst
it's true that I still love you,
I could find another one better and true, so
without further ado,
this is my breakup letter to you.
I'm sorry, but
find another man
to be greater than good to you!

Startling Truth

I never really liked her
like she loved me.
All that she did for me,
I would've never done for her,
whenever she would moan,
my heart would angrily groan,
I could've never felt complete with her
like she did with me, and
though I desired to be with her
for all eternity,
life would've never permitted me, because
she had broken so many hearts,
happy homes, and
karma once told me
that what goes around comes around, so
I was just her fate,
bringing her to a shocking reality
of all the evil things she once did.

The Old Apartment (After the Divorce)

(after the split)

It was a getaway spot
where the room temperature
stayed at 100 degrees beyond hot,
even though 'twas sometimes cold outside,
sex, sex, and more sex was an ongoing pleasure,
warming up the insides.

Slow music,
I couldn't disturb the already disturbed neighbors,
who watched me go and come
with different faces,
from all sorts of different places,
using them to close in on the empty spaces
that my old love had left me to endure.

lined up bottles,
ongoing parties,
countless text messages and phone calls,
dinner and movie dates,
thank goodness for no sex tapes,
this is the unforgettable yet regrettable shameful life,
lived at the old apartment.

Part 3

With Special Dedication 2 You!

Nana Teresa

(4 my Grandmother)

Beautiful queen of soul,
you are most precious
than gold, and
though to you
this world has been cold,
you're the only known soul
that life shouldn't scold.

Helena

(2 mother)

Life
came as a surprise 2 you,
especially when you
bore your first child,
so young and confused
with poverty and loneliness
faithfully by your side, but
through it all,
a true love sprung up inside,
not letting go of us, your pride,
even if it meant losing your life.
So,
whenever I think of a virtuous woman,
it is U that I first think of, because
loving me, and
being my mother,
has made me all of what I'm made of.
I Love U!

Queen Marie

(4 my daughter Anniyah Marie)

I can't call you beautiful,
for thou art not
what they are; beautiful.
Beautiful
is what everyone is, and
claims to be.
You are indeed
something far beyond beauty,
a Queen, an Idealist,
full of ingenuity, and
though still a child,
your cries make 4 me better company
than the words expressed today
in this world that surrounds me.

I love you!

◇◇◇◇◇◇◇◇◇◇◇

It was about noon. I was sitting in the front of my Stryker at an Iraqi Army base, which we used for an outpost. There had been an attack a few minutes earlier at the nearest Iraqi police station by the insurgents. It was a loud and somewhat brief moment. As I laid my seat back to relax for a few minutes, there were bodies of Iraqi Policemen being hauled on stretchers and in body bags. I couldn't help but think that one day that could be me. Moments later, the Iraqi police retaliated by burning down homes in the village, beating civilians and beheading a few.

So this poem came to me. I had an unborn child at home, and sometimes all that happened around me made it hard for me to think that I'd make it home. I started writing it but didn't complete it because we had to continue mission. When we got back to our base camp (FOB), there was a message written on the dry erase board. My daughter was born that day at 12:13 p.m. This is how the title "10/08/07" came about. It was seven days after my birthday, and I couldn't have asked for a better birthday present and a better relief after a hard day's work.

10/08/07
(Somewhere in the Desert, Iraq)

(4 my daughter)

Today was a beautiful day,
a day when love
brought me back from astray, and
though I wasn't there to see ur face,
I remembered
to get on my knees to say thanks and pray.

Welcome, Child,
into my life of calm and wild,
where peace deserves a home, but
agony and adversity dwells upon its throne, and
though it saddens me to be here alone,
it overwhelms me with joy
to hear your voice on the phone.

I pray that we'd be best of friends
as I perform my duties
to you as a dad
while you teach me to be a man.
And though,
I can't promise you forever great days,
I hope together, we can weather the storm,
no matter its size, shape, or form, so
on behalf of mama, Damien, and I,
Welcome, Child!

My Son and Me

(4 my son Damien)

My son and I are two, but
yet whole,
a love so real, we share,
warmth in times of cold,
a piece of my soul,
one of the best loves
I'm able to hold.

My son and I are two, but
yet whole!

Ethiopian Girls

(2 Baza and Maseret)

Timid, but
very outspoken in quietness,
your uniqueness and beauty
are far beyond what
I can imagine or see.
African,
that's what you are, but
you're more of a special star 2 me, because
I can see U from afar
whether or not ur in the dark.

A Rose By Any Other Name

Born beautifully a negro,
voice tender, sweeter than a sparrow,
her love is life's marrow,
a fragile heart full of grief, pain & sorrow,
Tommy calls her a slut,
Bobby calls her a whore,
Jamal calls her my nigger,
Marcy says she's a prostitute,
Mommy calls her worthless,
Daddy finger f——s her and
calls her a bitch, but
I call her a Rose,
A rose by any other name.

To Any Woman

I will forever write about a woman
for as long as I may live, because
in my eyes she'll always be the most beautiful of
humans, and
to us all, birth she painfully gave.

I will speak of a woman,
saying her name aloud yet softly
whether or not in my head,
African, American, Chinese or German, because
she is the backbone of me, when no one else cares.

I will forever love a woman,
spiritually pure or worldly as pearls, because
the existence of her
makes me complete as a MAN.

Caroline

(4 my friend Netzelia)

Always compared to Red wine,
sweet, hypnotic, and seductive,
your words have been my spine,
holding me up firmly
from time to time.

When life seemed hard, and
love became afraid,
your words gave me strength
as it dwelled in back of my head.

So
how could there be
a friend so genuine like you
in a world so filthy and cruel?

You give hope
to both worthy and unworthy hearts,
restoring faith in love
when heartbreak killed her all.

Lest no one say
you're not the truth, for
if anyone be true, then surely thee.
I've seen truth
and it's all because of you,
Caroline.

Women

Women bring men great joy, but
It's only after the sex
When men treat them like toys!

A Hero

(2 Dad)

No man I know
would stand so tall
against violence, poverty, and pain
when friends, family and enemies
prayed that you will fall,
not understanding the true significance
of you, your love, and
what it means to us all, but
now as poverty, violence and pain
taunts them,
on your name they call.
Like you,
some didn't have a father, so
Dad,
I will always love you, and
appreciate all that you give,
even if you or the world
considers it small.

Men

Men bring women great peace, but
It's only after we leave
that they worry and can't sleep.

Nothing Shall Come Between Us

(4 my mother)

Mother,
to thee, I've not been a natured son,
hovering between the crowd and home,
I felt that without you,
I'd be better off on my own.
But your love grew stronger,
sheltering me against evil and harm,
always welcoming me
to the home in your arms,
you are indeed highest amongst Women,
lovable as love can be, and
nothing nor can anyone prove otherwise.
I love U, and
Nothing shall come between us!

Kota J. Franklin

Teen Mother and Infant Child

I share the pain
in your eyes, because
it always makes me cry.
Mom and Dad are gone, and
there's no one by your side, but
open your heart, and
let that innocent infant love inside,
even though it seems
that every man is just another passer-by,
keep your head up, and
continue to strive, because
if there's one who unconditionally loves you,
then,
He sits up high

Kids

Other people's kids bring us great pride, but
It's only after "the one" is pregnant
When love is dispelled by strife!

Fallen

(a tribute 2 my fallen comrades)

Endless raindrops
cannot replenish the tears
I've shed.
The countless beautiful emotions
cannot soothe my soul
to ease the pain I bear.
You were everything
a man could ever be,
Heroes and Heroines,
who shared my broken dreams.
Your death,
didn't put an end to me,
it is your absence that
shatters my being,
making me feel as though
the air I breathe,
is breathed in vain.
And if this war we fight
shall one day make me deaf,
I will never forget
the beautiful sounds
of your unspoken names.
So lay in peace
my dear brothers and sisters, and
one day in the afterlife
we shall all meet again,

to rejoice in Freedom, Freedom, because
it is only then that the
Freedom for which we fight
will be Free!

Little Miss Sunshine

Bright corners, yet
darker than night
with little ones roaming and wandering
hoping to find someone
to scratch the itch
whether or not it's enough
for the rent or one dish.

Gotta make this paypa,
too much money in the gov'ment,
but too much crimes and wars
to pay for,
Gotta make it thru this life,
whether or not
it's around the pole, or
giving the sweet cum from her hole.

Sad it is, but
her life is a nightmarish dream
that her mama lives in reality, and
this is how she came into being,
being a human being,
being the queen of her streets, because
papa became her regular,
licked her honey, and
said she'd been well groomed
just like her mother.

Ghastly it is, but
who U know cares
to educate her,
house her,
better her,
and awaken her from her dream
to live beautifully as she is beautiful in reality.

Iraq

Oh
desert land,
where chaos and hatred stands,
come together as one,
2 speak tribal, cultural, and sexual equality
4 peace to understand.

Oh,
desert land of
spilled Innocent bloods,
countless flocks,
ripening crops,
religious wars,
come together,
sing beautiful melody in unison, and
know that there's one GOD, because
in HIS own likeness,
we were all created.

So,
beautiful desert land,
put down your arms,
and let freedom reign!

To My Muses (A Tribute)

If I succeed,
let it be known
that it wasn't on my own, because
without your unceasing support, and
continuous unconditional love shown,
I'd remain unknown.

If I fail,
let it be known,
that it wasn't a choice of mine, because
I strived to succeed from time to time,
whether or not
my ambitions, dreams, and goals were undermined.

But If die,
I beg of thee
not to weep, because
life wasn't promised unto me to keep, but
it was only you
that I live this life to please!

I love U!

Liberty

Why
does Liberty sit up high on her throne
watching our crimes and immoralities
when she should be here amongst us
to ensure that we live freely in equality, and
very peacefully?

Ms. Hollywood

(2 Hollywood celebrities)

Very appealing
to every man,
she lives in
a world of her own,
she holds company
with her own kind,
engages in relations
with those around her.
So very big,
Inexplicably small, sexy small, and
beautiful, but
conceited.

Lovebird

(2 one of God's wonderful creatures)

Oh beautiful lovebird
Humming sweet silent melody,
Sing to me a song of peace, and
Heal this mourning heart of mine
In its time of grief!

Oh beautiful lovebird,
Humming sweet silent melody,
Sing to me a song of grace, and
Calm this angry heart of mine
In this time of rage!

Oh beautiful lovebird,
Humming soothing silent melody,
Sing to me a song of love, and
Mend this broken heart of mine
And set me free when you fly by above!

Music

She once spoke to me
words that I had never
heard before,
words that are spoken
no more.
beautiful messages she told,
words gratifying to my soul, but
now,
music
makes me cold, because
nature and men,
it now scolds!

Some Model Chicks

So you possess a body
like that of a coke bottle,
at least that's what you're told.
From magazines, TV screens, and runways,
you walk with a scripted smile,
shrouding the emptiness you carry inside.
from continents to suites to mansions,
your have not a home, because
conceit has stolen your heart,
blinding you to who you were once before.
Pitiful it is, but
even those of the common status
matters to you no more!

Tobacco Junkies

I watch U daily
with much disgust and amazement
as U rot Ur teeth,
speaking with a fetid breath,
spending Ur last dime
on Grizzly,
Copenhagen,
Kools,
New Ports,
Carmel,
Cuban Cigars,
Miami,
Marlboros, and
so I wonder,
how long will it be
before the numerous deaths from Cancer
teach U a lesson?

Martin Luther King Jr., Rosa Parks

Your names speak a capella,
singing bravery like Mandela,
from the walls of White America
to the hearts of Black Africa.

Your names are hot,
burning up the issues of race,
like the early sunrise of Jamaica,
through the clear skies of Soweto.
Your names are fire!

Your names are freedom,
free like the passage of air,
Your names have paid my fare,
to vote and live peacefully in stardom!

Maya Angelou

You are queen of the soulful words
that live in me,
spoken through me,
empowering and uplifting
as life can be,
whether humorous,
serious, or
religious, because
every time I write,
your honor speaks through me.

Ghana in Virgin Skin

(4 my friend Ghana)

Ghana,
U are queen in a virgin skin,
appraised in all African Lands,
known as a goddess all over the world, because
U reign higher than Queen Elizabeth of England,
in all the beautiful Virgin Islands.
Everyone
who has seen thee
describes you as someone
with a persona humble and sweeter than peach, and
though I know you not,
when I look into your eyes,
with all honesty,
my heart and soul has to agree.
Wanting
to know you
is an honor of which I often think, because
I know that
just to feel the touch
of your smooth chocolate coated skin,
is a fantasy of which every man dreams.
Atlases, geographical encyclopedias,
Model magazines,
TV, or computer screens
cannot fully describe you.
Thus,

You are one in a million,
one of the truest of our kind.
You are a Woman, yet a Nation!
Ghana!

Internet Woman

Sometimes,
your company seems better than ecstasy
as I drowse in fantasies of your e-mail messages,
when hope eludes me.
Your photos depict
an image of you at best,
when half naked
with your hands covering just your breasts.
It's a sinful nature
to feel strong in my lower half
when looking at you, but
sometimes
when love leaves me to be alone
to fight against life on my own,
this is a feeling that gets me through.

Only if Life Were Color-Blind!
All about Noir

Dear Diary,
   How difficult is it to see
Something as simple as equality
   Something not very short of this known fact;
That we're all the same
   Though we wear different color skins?

Part 4

The Concept and Misconception of Life in Color

Change Unchanged

Change is here...we must still bear the unchanged
Black remains our skin...White is America's next
of kin.

I Know Not Thee, America

I know not thee, America.

Did you once long ago
hear about a woman named Africa,
whose heart was battered?
She toiled hot sands,
with chains locked to her hands,
sores planted beneath her feet,
trying to find a place to rest her womb,
as she carried me and my brothers across
the fields where there laid countless tombs.

I know not thee, America.

Did you once long ago
see a woman named Africa,
whose face was stained in tears?
She spoke in hoarse tones
trying to express her pain,
in a voice that only she could hear.
She sat face down on boats,
shivering from the chills of ocean waters,
traveling to a place she didn't know,
where she'd later bare me and my brothers,
to sustain ridicule and inequality.

Did you once hear her speak?
Oh mine, her voice was my only peace.
You speak of her somewhat, but
with much less admiration.
She told me
she once long ago met you
when you introduced yourself to her as Boss and Master,
holding a whip in your hands.

She told me
you're my father.
My first name is Africa, so
they call me African American!

But still,
I know not thee, America!

Redemption

Picture me rolling, a black man
down the white paved streets,
cruising through rich suburbs
unafraid of my mind to think,
my tongue to speak or
what my soul may feel.

I could yell
from the peak of Everest, and
be heard from below the Pacific,
dream of Martin Luther King Jr. as president,
saying, "Let freedom reign"
singing the po' boy blues,
wanting to kiss the lips
of the white goddesses and queens, because
a slave will no longer be my name,
racism will no longer be a game, and
the gospel will bring a mocked man no shame.

I can hear my Miranda Rights
unread by a gun,
as though putting up a fight
whether it's broad day or
darker than night.
I can be me,
a negro black man,
saying "Hi" to white folks

without their purse
tightly held in their hands
or underneath their arms.

I can be freely loved
by a white girl/woman
without her being
humiliated as a nigger lover, because
love has no color
just as I know Jesus
as a loving man not colored.

I can be me,
just a negro black man, but
equally powerful
like the redneck white man!

I can be me,
a negro black man.

Untitled

Sometimes I wish
the world was color blind so
that every race
will dwell freely in the same place,
voiding the oppression of minds.
loving us as one; mankind,
treating everyone as equals
without freedom being impartial.
But then I dreamed that someday
there would be love
where there was once hate.
Someday,
there will be peace
where there was once rage.
Someday,
there will be laughter
where there was once distress.
Someday,
there will be acceptance
where there was once neglect.
Someday,
there will be justice
where there was once injustice.
Someday
there will be Emancipation
where there was once captivity.
Someday

there will be Unity
were there was once racial Partiality.
Someday
there will be a will
where there was once a wish.
And someday,
there will be Reality
where there was once a dream; this dream!

Angry

I'm angry,
angry that after 250 years
racism still seems to exist.

I'm angry,
angry that though the rich get richer,
poverty still roams the streets
while starvation taunts the poor.

I'm angry,
angry that though Ms. Justice and Mr. Law
an innocent black man still gets sent to jail, but
to liberate and free the whites,
they never fail.

I'm angry,
angry that blacks hate blacks, and
the only time we seem to unite
is at the million man's march.

Can We Laugh, America?

(4 us COLOR)

For centuries,
we've endured pain, and
taught to cry, but
for how much longer,
must we, color,
strive for impunity?

Can we laugh, America,
tortured memories
abide about our heads,
restless days and sleepless nights,
threading together a nation
in which we're unappreciated,
niggers are what we've become, for
equality isn't today, tomorrow, and
perhaps never.

Dim Lightened,
the sun of our lives sets away,
in a place where our race
isn't and was never a slave, and
here is where we should call home, but
we're separated as if in a tomb,
with rights taken, and
limited privileges given.

Can we laugh, America, and
wipe away our endless tears,
mend our broken pieces
to live as one,
before this life of ours
is long gone, for
America is us all?

Change

In the heat of Africa
where the sun beams on gravel,
I saw no black or white
until later, when, to America I traveled.
I thought it was paradise,
the land where all dreams came true, but
now I see inequality leading me to my demise,
as I hope that liberty and justice will one day be prude.

A Negro Speaking

There is a better tomorrow,
    free of ridicule for me, a negro,
death, tears and pain will be no more.
There is a better tomorrow.

There will be a better tomorrow,
    free from the belittlement for me, a nigger,
equality will be the core of the existence of men, and
I say,
There will be a better tomorrow.

There is a better future for US Color,
    whether toned as caramel, white, or black,
love shall fill the air,
beautifully like the still wind at dawn,
did you hear me,
There is a better tomorrow.

Diverse Memories

What I remember of yesterday's life,
innocent losses, nightmares, genocide,
taunting her, Africa
besetting her with colorful lies.

What I remember of yesterday's life,
hard work days, massive whips, and unceasing pain
building her, America,
spotlighting her for all her gains.

What I remember of yesterday's life,
limited education, ignorance, and illiteracy
describing her, Africa
though denied help, forcing her to endure poverty.

What I remember of yesterday's life,
unlimited education, noble suites, and mansions
abounding her, America
bringing forth, her, to be this great shameful nation.

What I remember of tomorrow's life,
heavenly days with harmony to embrace,
where her race, African,
living freely, dreaming beautifully in an immortal place.

Black Man (Un Homme Noir)

I'm a black man,
yes I am, and
on peace is where I stand.

I'm a black man,
yes I am, and
divine strength is my hands.

I'm a black man,
yes I am, and
equality is all I demand, for
racism and hate,
I cannot withstand!

What Is It?

What is it
This bondage that we live in
Where our eyes are void of tears,
Unable to express our own fears?

What is it
The bondage that we love in
Where love is an ordeal, and
A man's heart is incapable to feel?

What is it
The bondage that we run from
When the freedom that we aspire
Isn't everyman's truest desire?

What is it
The bondage that we speak of
When our speech is full of hate,
And everyone's heart expresses insipidity?

What is it
The life that we live,
When, to the poor,
We cannot freely give, and
The simplest things in life we cannot appreciate?

What is it
The joy that we beseech
When a simple prayer
Our tongues cannot speak?

What If

(a trivia 'bout life)

What if
death was your best friend?
How many lives would you
encourage him to take?

What if
love was the only word
in the dictionary?
How would you define it?

What if
the Bible was the only knowledgeable book,
the love novel, the encyclopedia, the history book
to read and learn?
How many of us would devote ourselves to education?

What if
sex was the only crime punishable by death
that a man could commit?
How many of us would abstain ourselves from it?

What if
love was the priciest yet scarcest thing?
How much would you be willing to pay, or
how far would you go to find it?

What if
loneliness was your worst fear?
How many of your enemies
would you be willing to reconcile with
in order to have company?

Yesterday, Today, Tomorrow

Yesterday,
    full of evil and devilish deeds.
Today,
    full of tears, murderous crimes and economic greed.
Tomorrow,
    full of joy, everlasting joy, freedom, peace, and memories to keep.

Yesterday,
    consumed by darkness.
Today,
    empowered by race.
Tomorrow,
    equality shall be appraised in every place.

Yesterday,
    Today, and
    Tomorrow!

Africa

Mama once told me
of the beauty and love you possess, and
since the day I inhaled my first scent of you and breathed,
I've cherished that beauty and love in my head.

Most beautiful,
the oldest of many sisters,
you are my Cinderella,
a once long ago goddess now made a slave.

Thus,
though forced to fall at the feet of the richest,
while enduring the unending murder of your sons &
daughters,
your tears of bravery, and
courage to rise
makes you a true mother amongst them all,
the best of the best, and
I love U!

I Am an African

I was born in Liberia
to the melody of screaming guns
where long hot walks,
soccer, schools, and soil toiling
are activities of fun,
like surfing, four-wheeling or
tanning on flat roofs in the American sun.
I Am An African.

I wear black like panther,
possess the strength of a lion,
the voice of a sparrow,
the cry of a wolf,
the sprint of a cheetah,
the hair of a lamb,
the wings of an eagle,
the thirst of an elephant,
the humping of rabbits,
make love better than Kama Sutra,
I Am An African!

You can call me
Emmanuel, Jésus,
Mandela, Martin, Gandhi, Malcolm, Kenya, Zimbabwe,
Ethiopia, Egypt, Malawi,
Senegal, Congo, Ghana, Sudan
Nigeria, Guinea, Mozambique.

I speak French,
Swahili, Creole, English,
I was born in Liberia,
I Am An African!

Life

This life is fun,
oh so funny,
that I'd love to laugh, but
all I can ever do is cry!

This life is short,
oh so short,
that, to the end,
with time, I'd love to crawl, but
all I can ever do is walk!

This life is a gift; priceless,
oh so free,
that I'd love to live wherever I please, but
I've yet to find a place
Where there's no crime of race,
poverty, everlasting freedom, and peace!

This is life,
so fun, short, and free!

Killing Me Softly

This world
is killing me softly,
slowly,
with unspoken words,
unending oppressive pain.
I can't feel the sun,
or appreciate the moon.
Nature
sits beneath her throne,
as liberty
dies from race and creed,
yet I remain this breed
endlessly striving to succeed
in my colored world of inferiority.
This world
is killing me softly,
slowly,
my mind's tearful words
now sounds like gibberish
as they fall on the ears of the average,
rich, poor, stereotypical beings,
to whom the act of helping or listening
has no gain, because
the poor heart of the wealthy,
most powerful said beings,
has no appeal, and
is unable to feel.

This world
is killing me softly,
slowly,
so living just to die
frightens me no more, because
I'll be all I can be,
striving for a change,
while, accepting my fate
as a black man,
darker than an ore.
This world
is killing me softly,
slowly...

Daybreak

Horns blearing,
school buses filled in diversity
with happy and frowned faces,
lawns mowing,
music screaming,
eggs, grits, sausage, French toast cooking,
the homeless relocating,
the poor still suffering,
the rich still earning,
the dealers stashing,
the cops wrongfully killing,
protecting, serving and arresting,
the media lying,
the collectors calling and collecting,
death taking;
if only in Genesis
the devil didn't tempt and deceive,
we'd be in a Garden
living with sanity, because
tomorrows would bring no worries!

Life #2

Take my hands and never let go,
so that over death, I'll have eternal control.
Take the hands of time and stand still,
so that you and I will never grow old.

Trick and Treat / Whores and Pimps

I don't know,
5, 10, maybe 20
will give u plenty
of anything except true company.

Where;
back seats, corners, motels, hotels, parks, anywhere,
to uncover and discreet the deeds of night,
for only 5, 10, 20, maybe homicide,
without a formal burial,
leaving a weeping mother,
a cold case, no murder trial.

Peace of Mind

We search for mental relaxation,
peace of mind,
scrambling through thoughts
from our pieces of mind,
that highlights old and new times,
painful and laughing times.

We search for mental relaxation,
peace of mind,
kneeling to manifest our humanness
from discos to private shrines,
for past dedication, addiction
to evil,
for it seemed righteous in our small minds.

We search for mental relaxation,
peace of mind,
trying to understand the wonderment
in the smiles of the blind, because
we too live in perpetual darkness,
struggling to shine,
as we become pimps and concubines.

It's funny,
we possess bland souls, but
we search for mental relaxation,
peace of mind.

Mirror/Review Yourselves

It is daily
that a man/woman complains, and
counts gloomy days,
it is daily
that a man/woman recalls
many evil ways, but
it isn't daily
that a man/woman sits to count his blessings,
it isn't daily
that a man/woman is thankful
for the air he/she is breathing,
it isn't daily
that a man/woman helps another
without the anticipation of receiving.
it is daily that death moves fearlessly
with the intention of killing, and
it is daily that death
fulfills his addiction by taking, but
the only problem is that
this is a lesson 'bout life, taught daily,
from which we aren't learning.

My Good-Bye Letter

Dialla Province
Fob Warhorse (Ba'Qubah, Iraq)
Apo, Ae 09336

May 27, 2008

Dear Mr. Army:

Thanks for the long four years we spent together. I've become a better person than I once was; disciplined, tolerant, and focused. I know you, and I could never be friends again, but memories of you will always live in my head. We had some crazy times together, especially when we fought and saw death together. I remember when we used to party hard, until I lost my first marriage when I crashed in life's fast lane. You are also one of the main reason that I am a citizen of this great country for which we fight. There were plenty of times when I thought that I wouldn't live to write this letter, but now the time has come for us to part. There are other things in life that I feel are more important, and I'd like to see what the world of normality has to offer. I have kids now, and I'm happily remarried, so I'd love to dedicate my full time to my family.

Nevertheless, the fact that others may regard you as a jail cell of torture, while others may regard you as paradise on earth, I see you to be something different.

I know not how to describe it, but I must let you know that you're just like everyone else with flaws, ups and down. You were a good friend who got me started in life to achieve some of what I have achieved. You were also a friend who stood in the way of certain goals that I had to accomplish. I have nothing against you, so as you and the rest of our fellow comrades stay in arms, I'll continuously pray for your strength and lasting success. Thanks for everything.

Yours truly,
Soldier

Part 5

It's Just Life, Not a Just Life, but It's My Life!

The Waiter

Amidst
kings and queens,
gods and goddesses,
celebrities, common or wealthy,
on haute-cuisines they dine,
with expensive wines,
smelling of eucalyptus,
two or three at a time,
a dozen snob, and
because of my abandonment to poverty,
on them,
I'm waiting.

Yearning
for pleasant love, unconditional,
healing from heartbreaks,
eradicating loneliness,
on her, my love,
I'm waiting.

Living,
in peace, painfully,
poverty and suffering,
hoping hopelessly,
striving for redemption,

struggling to endure inequality,
praying for endless tomorrows of joy,
on death,
I'm Waiting.

I

I
will love
you,
him,
her,
we are all human beings.

I
will praise/appreciate
the moon,
sun,
air,
life,
death,
nature,
these are all heavenly things,

I will praise
Him,
He made me!

I
will write
words,
music,
poetry,

scripts,
novels,
these will express my acuity.

I
will teach
the gospel,
creation,
evolution,
history,
these are all misinterpreted facts.

I
will be
Me,
this is all I know to be!

Independent Me (Only I)

Why must my tears
fall in twos
when it is I alone
who shed them?
Why must my heart
bear a love for two or more,
when it is I alone
who unconditionally loves me?
Why must I walk in fear
amongst beasts and men
when it is I that I fear?
Only I,
independent me,
Only I
to bear my pain,
Only I
to pay 4 my sins,
Only I
to appreciate me,
Only I
to be me,
Only I
to lose my soul,
Only I
to make me whole.
It's only I
that can stay true to me,

in all the good and bad
that I do,
Only I,
independent me.

Greed

I want to be free
just like the "white" on their skins.
I want to be him
suave and witty with words.
I want to be loved
just like the pleasure of sexual desires.
I want to be him,
wanted by every species that breathes.
I want to be rich,
just like the unending values of monies, but
I want to remain me
simple as simplicity can be.

A Lone Soldier

To most of the world,
I'm all I can be
as I wear this uniform
walking, riding and shaking hands through the streets,
but
inside me,
I'm nothing, because
of the choices I've made.
I'm alone
a lone soldier,
constantly running from my fears,
fighting away my tears,
trying to fill the emptiness in my soul.
The light of the day
means nothing to me, for
all my eyes can see is night,
darkness full of nightmares,
evil has exhausted my sight, and
everything right seems so wrong, and
everything wrong seems so right.

To most of the world,
I've done nothing but great things,
paying for the cause of freedom,
giving my life in the place of their own, but
inside me,
I see no good,

I'm alone,
a lone soldier,
trying to escape every sound,
constantly judging the differences and similarities
of those that surrounds me,
fighting paranoia,
trying to find evil in every man, but
it is I that evil dwells within, and
everything normal seems so abnormal, and
everything abnormal seems so normal, and
though it is peace that I fight for,
peace abides not with me.
Sometimes I wish that my soul would freeze, so
my heart can feel no more pain, because
it is freedom that I fight for, but
freedom has yet to set me free, and
it tears me apart
that your eyes are unable to see, for
I'm alone,
A Lone Soldier.

Brain Dead

I see,
But my eyes have no sight, because
Corruption and violence has corrupted by vision.

I feel,
But my heart is void of feelings, because
Evil has enticed my heart and turned me cold.

I hear,
But my sense of hearing is dead, because
I'm a victim of war, and
Guns and mournful cries are all I ever hear.

I smell,
But my sense of smelling is of no good,
Because the horrible smell of corpses and this sinful
world
Has invaded my smell.

I speak,
But I can no longer talk, because
Perversity and vulgarity have corrupted my speech

I taste,
But I can no longer eat, because
Agony, depression and stress have seized my appetite.

If I Had Wings

If I had wings
beneath my arms,
I'll set out and away
to find my heart's lucky charm.

I was once a happy man
smiling and grinning at everything I saw,
until the only woman I loved
set out away with an unknown man,
leaving my veins without a pulse.

If I had wings
beneath my feet,
I'd set out and away
to find my mind's eternal peace.

I was once a happy child,
rolling, crawling, and walking with innocence and
happiness
until the stages of life
brought me stress in abundance as though affectionate
blessings.

If I had wings
beneath my arms,
I'll set out and away
to find the most peaceful dwelling
which the wise calls the Heavens!

A Lesson Untaught

I should be love…and be loved, because
I would wound the unfaithful, and
delight the loving to love more.

I should be words…and be spoken,
freely worded, because
I would unthinkingly, fearlessly condemn the wicked,
and
appraise, glorify, and acknowledge the intelligent and
sound minds.

I should be sight…and be seen, because
I would blind, and disdain the perverse, and
appreciate the beauty of the beautiful,
nature, God's creation.

I should be sex…and be sexed, because
I would sicken the promiscuous, pussyfooters, prosti-
tutes, and
bestow passion to spark the fire of a dying Romance,
especially if done under the oath of Holy Matrimony…

I should be life…and be lived, because
I would stress the hearts of undeserving souls, and
give wings of success, happiness, and offspring
to the ones who treat me like gold.

I should be death…and be feared, because
I would take away the breath of the illegal addicts, the sinful, and
let live the meek, righteous, godly, and those grateful
of my sister Life, my father God, and
all that they freely give!!

Image

(autobiographical)

I've grown
to become a man
from the happiest poor boy
that I could've ever been.
My words
are no more stuttering, and
love,
my heart is now mastering.
Life
in the past
as my infant child
was a boogie monster
like dark closets
are to little boys, but
as the guns continued to speak,
papa sold tire-like slippers
for mama to buy affordable diapers, and
a pack of red boxed candles
so that there was always light
for me not to lose my way.
I would watch the neighbors' kids
run naked in the cold, cold rain
while mama sat on the back porch
selling sardines
in order for me to one day have a brain.
A not so ordinary child

is who I once was, but
I grew up in a wonderful family
who loved each other without cause, and
though now I'm just another colored man,
these are facts
that I'd like history to know to say
just encase she ever writes about me.

Success

I live 4 success,
4 failure is my only enemy, so
in this world of dire and stress,
my life about all things
must indeed progress!

I live 4 success,
4 ambition is my only friend, so
in this world of knowledge and press,
to succeed is not a wish, but
more of a strive to me!

I live 4 success,
and not to gain the best of fame,
4 if the world never learns my name,
it won't afflict upon me any pain
as it would if I never succeed!

Prisoner of War (Liberia/Iraq)

I am a
Prisoner of War,
though not physically
restrained behind bars.
My name is a victim of trauma,
my body tattooed in scars,
War is all I know,
though my words
may not let it show, but
the air I now still breathe
gives my life its inner glow.
I am a
Prisoner of War,
death is all I've seen,
both innocent, consequential, and unforeseen, but
the presence of God in me
makes my life sane,
giving me opportunities
to dream beautiful peaceful dreams!

Dead Poets' Society

There stands the stage,
a microphone,
drum sets,
pianos, and
guitars, but
the poet,
his poetry;
no more soothing,
appeasing,
elating,
inspiring,
intriguing,
enthralling,
speaks without rhythm,
his words have grown old
as he aged,
profanity spills out, because
it's the only way he knows how
to express himself,
his rage,
conveying the everyday activities,
racial, sexual, and religious discrimination, and
the violence and lies on the front page, because
in his heart,
love has lost her home.

After I Die

On the morning after I die,
the blue, dark, and clear skies will cry
in my absence by their sides, but
if in an instinct I'm forgotten,
that'd be no surprise, because
I live visible amongst men, but
treated as though I wore a disguise.

Cold

(4 my heart)

Why
must my heart be
humble and forgiving
when betrayal and loss
are the worst pain I ever feel,
shattering every component
of my life,
without a chance to heal?

Void

Who am I
supposed to be?
What is it
that my heart is meant to feel?
What is it
that my eyes are meant to see
when my heart is void of everything—
love, hate, passion, compassion, and peace?
When all I know is Solipsism?

Weary (Enigma)

I'm weary,
stripped of dignity,
leased to pain
leashed to poverty,
there's no equality,
hate is tranquility,
peace is insanity,
death is impunity.

I'm weary,
unloved by love,
leased to heartbreak,
leashed to loneliness,
hope is hopeless,
there's no us, we, or you,
I'm on my own,
A man scorned.

I'm weary
struggling to struggle,
abandoned by destiny,
humans are now commodities,
ruled in sovereignty,
birth is a catastrophe,
there is no us, we, or you,
I'm on my own,
A man scorned.

Fear

Mama,
take my hands.
Protect me from evil men,
as though still in your womb.
I'm now a man, but
defenseless as though a child.
Papa,
walk along side me
through these violent, hateful streets,
as though still seated up high
on your shoulders.
I'm now a man, but
defenseless as though a child.
I'm afraid of him; poverty,
I'm afraid of he; love,
I'm afraid of them; lies and segregation.
I'm afraid of this place,
and every race.
Come and take me home,
I thought I was old enough
to be on my own, but
now it dawns to me,
that it's hard being out here alone.

Me

My name is Me,
pleasant as could ever be, and
though on the cover of magazines,
newspapers or TV screens
I can't be seen,
my contentment is a wonderment
that lives in my heart, and
that's the joy of Me, because
unlike many,
I'm able to accept and enjoy simplicity.

Unfaithful

Mind,
why must you leave me
to fantasize about a love
that is not mine,
dreaming and hoping
2 share such a love one day in time?
Eyes,
why must you leave me
to look lustfully
at another one's love,
penetrating her clothing
to see her chest, and
picturing in between
the meet of her thighs?
Hands,
why must you touch me
to make me feel lustful passion
of what my mind has
imagined and dreamed,
what my eyes have seen and hope to see,
everything that's not for me.
Me,
why must I be unfaithful?

1984

(an autobiography)
Sweet, 1984,
I remember
not much of you, for
innocent was I,
breathing thin air.
I knew not its origin,
crying the tears,
I knew not its cause.

You left me
for 2 years and
a century,
between the claws of life,
to grow and understand
the essence of nature's air,
to experience
love, joy, hate, and pain,
the reasons for the tears
I shed, and
to make decisions
that will lead me
to an untimely or timely death.

Oh how I wish
to be once more, a child,
when my mind could think

of thoughts I couldn't analyze, and
dream of dreams
I wouldn't understand, for
whenever life becomes unkind to me,
sometimes I wish
you never came.

Prodigal Me

Astray in evil,
in my tears,
I lay my head
with fears cast upon my bed.

Tomorrow,
so bright yet narrow,
the memories
of beautiful yesterday yet painful,
shadows my heart with unfading sorrow.

Peace,
is indeed all that I seek,
with the treasures of this world
in my bosom to keep, and
though surrounded by humans and friends,
without a home and love,
I'll always be that lost sheep.

But Hope,
is the woman of whom I dream
praying that someday
Her true love
will come and rescue me, and
deliver me to her, my love,
my one and only destiny.

Insomnia (Iraq)

Long days and nights of emptiness,
tiresome activities,
my body aches,
eyes bloodshot red,
darkness feels like day,
day like darkness,
sleep scowls at me,
deserting my need for her,
weeks are now months,
months are now years,
years are now decades,
decades are now centuries,
I lay abed
twitching from fatigue
troubling my veins, and
still I'm unable to sleep!

Routine Army (Iraq)

Fob Normandy (February '08)
Every morning I wake up,
as early as 1, 2, or 3,
eyes burning,
body half asleep,
immobile,
for a moment I can't speak.
The same old faces
walk pass my bunk,
speaking loudly
the same old corny jokes
over coffee,
the air smells like cigarettes, and
when I do get up,
I feel so much closer to cancer,
weakly putting on my uniform,
stringing my boots,
unconsciously walking to the bathroom
just to hurriedly shave and brush my teeth
in order to make it to the mission's brief,
listening to the same old speech, and
because of the job we do,
driving up and down Iraq,
looking for bombs on her streets,
I sometimes feel so close to death,
knowing that out there somewhere
it seeks and awaits me

or a member of my crew, so
I ask to bow our heads while
I pray saying,
"Thank U, Lord, for this day,
thank U for life and strength, and
I pray that as we leave here
to carry out another mission,
U will go with us
to guide and protect us, and
bring us back safe.
I pray that U will give our leaders
the knowledge they need
to make the right decisions and
lead us through.
We thank U,
We love U,
in Ur Holy Name I Pray.
Amen!"

Fame Awaits Me

Sweetheart,
you're cute,
more beautiful than most,
at least that's what you've been told,
so you think highly of yourself,
besetting everyone else, because
he said you have some potential.
Girl, don't be a swine,
reevaluate your traveling time
into destiny's arms,
there's still a long way to go, and
though you think lowly of me,
I know fame awaits me!

See,
I come from afar,
with so long to go,
from war's claws to peace's throne,
treading the soil of Africa
to singing the songs of America,
envisioning a dream for me,
putting first His holy name,
in order to get where I wanna be, because
fame awaits me!

It's not really about the fame,
or the love of money, because

unlike you and the others,
I don't want paparazzi to complicate me, but
to eradicate my hurt and pain
in order for my heart to sustain her love,
cherishing the air that I breathe, because
my long term dream
will be living a favored life of reality.
So now I say remember me, because
Fame awaits me!

My dude,
I didn't know you spit
your lyrics is so sick,
you'll be the next king of remix,
at least that's what you've been told,
so you forgot the look of the common faces, but
don't be a snob,
reevaluate your pathway
into destiny's arms, because
there is still a long way to go, and
though you may berate me,
I know fame awaits me!

Fame awaits me!

Misunderstood

I said
she was shinier than the sun,
so elegant and sophisticated in her being,
intelligent than the most I've seen, and
that I love her, but
she stood away from me,
wondering in disbelief,
asking me
what it was that I wanted from her, because
she felt that I just wanted to get in between.
She misunderstood.

She said
I had a nice car,
shinier rims than most she'd seen,
always dress nice with a fitted hat to match,
she wanted to be with me,
no strings attached, and
I knew she was go getta, but
now I thought she was just a gold digger,
trying to stay around for my chedda.
I misunderstood.

I said
she wore some black trousers
with some matching sneakers, and
they stood there and laughed at me,

calling me an old timer,
asking me where I was from, because
I didn't say black pants
with some matching shoes.
I guess those are words
that modern people use no more.
They misunderstood.

I Might Be, Maybe

Whimsical
is what I think I am, and
though sometimes described negatively,
positive
is what I am.
They call me many names, because
of my somber complexion,
a nigger, negro, nigga, African, and
for this, they sometimes despise my presence,
pointing fingers, throwing spit at me,
whether or not I smell of expensive fragrance.
They call me many names, because
of my dream of success,
ambitious, knowledgeable, strong, rich, and
for this, I have many friends,
some of whom are loyal,
while others just want to taste of fame.
They call me many names,
because of envy,
liar, cheater, promiscuous,
sometimes a square, but
she still adores me,
calling me perfect, loving,
caring, understanding, handy,
true, a realist, yet an enigma, so
to all of the above, I say,
I might be, maybe.

I Love Me Some…

I love me some regal woman,
high qualities adorned,
intelligent speech,
erotic appearance,
I love me some regal woman.

I love me some soldier girl,
high qualities adorned,
phenomenal,
goal achiever,
sex anytime girl,
I love me some soldier girl.

I love me some model chick,
high qualities adorned,
beauty undefined,
coke bottled body,
smooth textured skin,
twisted walk,
health freak,
I love me some model chick.

I love me some country girl,
high qualities adorned,
accented speech,
a wonderful mother,
a great cook like none other,
I love me some country girl.

The Forgotten

I shine bright like yellow,
bleeding brighter and darker than red,
carrying a black on my skin,
screaming louder than a fast moving train, but
you wear sun shades
to avoid my bright glow,
you keep distant to avoid seeing me bleed,
you wear white
just to be the opposite of me,
you wear head phones,
bebopping your head
to avoid listening to my heart groan in pain!

Conscious

Sometimes
when I take a look at life,
I often cry,
wondering why
we live in an open world
with so many closed hearts,
visible as lights, but
still can't be seen by the naked eyes
especially if you aren't yet a star.
Why
do we live in a full world
with so many empty minds,
speaking unceasingly of love, but
hating us mercilessly,
especially when criticizing He who sits above
as though the evil of our lives were his fault?
Why
do we expect more from life
when we treat her carelessly,
as though fortune were promised to us all
even if we didn't strive?

Evolution

I was a child…Innocent.
Everyone wanted to hold me.
Cute and adorable is what they called me.

I was an adolescent…Puberty.
I became aware of nature, and
began to develop the quest
to explore the desires of my manhood.
Charming is what they called me.

I was a teenager…Maturity.
I had somewhat tasted of life's many offers.
Women became very important,
especially the pleasure they could bring.
I began to court them, and
handsome is what I became.

I am an adult…Life/Responsibilities.
I've been held,
I've explored my curiosity,
I've tasted all of life's good and harsh times,
I've courted women, and
enjoyed all the pleasures they can possibly bring,
one, two, or three at a time, but
I've stopped to better myself for success, because
there are now lots of responsibilities, and

life is the only thing that I have, but
don't own, so I've gotta make the best of it.
A man is what they call me.

As I Am

I'm living,
in a world of many things inappropriate,
living in a world
where 'loving truly',
is no longer a man's priority,
living in a world
full of gloomy days,

I'm living,
living an imperfect life,
for I'm no angel, but
just a man.

Part 6

The Alpha and Omega,
the Beginning and the End,
the King of Kings

I Love U

(2 God)

I know
of many love stories,
have written many love poems,
loved unconditionally to be
unconditionally loved,
I've lost love,
hoping to find a better love, but
all of this love
compares not to thee at all.
Your love loves all,
a love that's so unconditional, so
unconditionally,
I Love U!

I Uphold Thee

Jesus,
I uphold thee, because
in all the earth,
I've met no such great King.

Jesus,
I uphold thee, because
in all my life,
I've befriended no such loyal friend.

Jesus,
I uphold thee,
in the beginning and end of time,
there shall be no one as true as thee.

Jesus,
I uphold thee,
above all and everyone, because
you're the only friend, brother, and father I desire
to keep.

Jesus,
I uphold thee,
so in all my trails and times of perseverance,
don't turn thy back away from me.

Jesus,

I uphold thee,
and no matter life's pleasures or pain,
It's thee whom I shall love for all eternity.

Jesus,
I uphold thee,
no matter my destiny,
with you is where I desire to be!

Jesus and the Gospel

Oh,
Thou art mighty, and
though some
rebel against thee,
berate thee,
call thee a myth,
in thee,
I have faith,
to teach me,
lead me,
speak to me, and
give me
the air I breathe.

Almighty King

It bothers me
that in so many words, and
with so many talents,
our hearts cannot worship thee.
I know,
that's its only U, Lord
that gives our hearts peace, so
please forgive our sins,
and set us free.

Above All

Above all,
I place thee first, for
without you,
my life is cursed.

Above all,
I place you up high,
without my belief in you,
I can never live there with you beyond the skies.

Above all,
you are the best,
without your presence in my heart,
my soul has no rest.

Above all,
you are the king, and
no matter where we find ourselves in this world,
your love and lordship will always reign!

Show Me

Show me
how to be a good man.
Help me fully understand
all that I have to do to be one with U.
Show me
how to be a Christian friend.
Show me
how to teach others
all the things of wrong nature, because
they aren't like U.
Show me
how to love faithfully,
to sincerely cherish the one you've given me
even if my worldly desires aren't pleased.
Show me,
Lord,
show me,
so that when I die,
I'll forever reside with U.

POS

I am,
a Prisoner Of Sin,
born of immorality,
victim of this world,
full of iniquity
a believer, but
not a doer.

I am
a Prisoner of Sin,
full of love and hate,
with no direction,
stumbling across life,
trying to fulfill
my sinful needs,
peer pressured by
both friends and foes.

I am
a Prisoner of Sin,
looking for peace, and
trying to honor my soul!

Thank You

Thank You
for watching over me
at night when I lay.

Thank You
for waking me up daily, and
setting me on my way.

Thank You
for hearkening your ears unto my words
whenever I get on my knees and pray.

Thank You
for keeping me on the right path
whenever I tend to go astray, and

Thank You
for coming into my life, and
I hope you stay.

Jesus, U R My Everything

As the sun
slips into the dusky clouds,
beckoning night to fall,
I'll whisper Ur name
in remembrance of what
it means me, because
U are my Light.

As the final air
bleeds from my nostrils
beckoning life to escape me,
I'll whisper Ur name
in remembrance of what
it means to me, because
U are my Life and Resurrection.

As friends neglect me,
beckoning loneliness to convict me,
I'll whisper Ur name
in remembrance of what
it means to me, because
U are my only true Friend.

And
as the world comes to an end
while judgment awaits every man,
I'll whisper U name

in remembrance of what
it means to me, because
U are the only way to Eternity.

Jesus,
U R my Everything.

Dear God

Please bless my heart
in its state of vulnerability,
forgive my mind
for its thoughts of immorality, because
despite my continuous efforts to change,
Your laws, I habitually
knowingly or unknowingly infringe.

Still I Breathe

(Iraq, Aug. 24, 2007, 8:09 a.m.)

Neatly
dressed in armor plates,
carrying loaded magazines
with a gun strapped to my chest,
fearless amongst savages,
I'm still defenseless, but
because of You, Lord,
still I breathe.

Death
knocked on my door this morning
sooo bright and early,
certain to take me away,
so that my enemies may have victory, but
You intervened and rescued me, and
though to themselves,
many now give the glory to be alive, because
of You, Lord,
still I breathe!

Thank U for loving me.
Thank U for saving me.
Thank U for parenting me.
Thank U, Lord, because
of You,
still I breathe.

A Brief Testimony

After spending fourteen unforgettable months in Iraq, this is something that I must share with you. It is a testimony that shall always be a part of me, and will always guide me through this life.

For fourteen months, we looked for and destroyed bombs, which are commonly known as IEDs/EFPs. During our missions, we were successful majority of the time, whereas some of the time we took blasts to our vehicles, injuring personnel. But through it all, we sustained no loss of life in our company. And this is one of the reasons for which I write this, because I'm very thankful.

However, I became directly involved in combat with the enemy on August 24, 2007 at 08:09 a.m. when my vehicle was bombed with one of the deadliest bombs made in the province of Iraq in which I served. Up till today's date, the only known explanation for why I survived that blast is because of God. A fellow soldier came up to me that night and said, "Man, I'm not religious, but after seeing you survive that hit, I know that there is a God somewhere." Due to this blast, one of my fellow soldiers riding with me received a purple heart medal because of injuries sustained during the hit. But overall, everyone was okay to go back to work the following day.

On March 18, 2008, I received another blast to my truck while carrying out a clearance mission. It was an underbelly, which hit directly beneath the center of the vehicle, injuring the TC or vehicle commander, my platoon sergeant, and the rear hatch gunner. The TC sustained a knee injury which put him out of the fight for the remaining two months of our tour. The platoon sergeant sustained a hit to his left leg causing him to lose feelings in that leg. He was also put out of the fight for the remaining two months of our tour. The rear hatch gunner sustained an injury which caused him to lose feeling in his face, and also his balance. He was out of the fight for a few weeks to a month. He returned to the fight and completed the last month. I on the other hand was put out of the fight for three days because of a minor hit to my head. I returned to the fight after my time of decompression and completed our two months of tour successfully. Thank God for his continuous blessings and mercy. I'm very grateful. There were many other hits in the rest of my company, with many different injuries. At the end of the tour, we found more IEDs, than they found us.

I'd also like to dedicate this part of the book to the twelve guys who had to leave the battlefield to return home to recover, after receiving numerous of hits and sustaining different injuries.

Part 7

Bible Verses that Got Me through Combat

2 Samuel 22:4

"I will call on the Lord, who is worthy to be praised: so shall I be saved from my enemies."

Psalm 50:23

"Whoso offereth praise glorifieth me: and to him that orderth his conversation aright will I show the salvation of God."

Psalm 91

"He that dwelleth in the secret
place of the Most High
shall abide under the shadow of the
Almighty.
I will say of the Lord
He is my refuge and m fortress:
my God; in Him will I trust.
Surely He will deliver thee from the
snare of the fowler,
and from the noisome pestilence.
He shall cover thee with His feathers,
and under His wings shalt thou trust:
his truth shall be thy shield and
buckler.
Thou shalt not be afraid for the
terror by night;
nor for the arrow that flieth by day;
nor for the destruction that wasteth
at noonday.
A thousand shall fall at thy side,

and ten thousand at thy right hand;
but it shall not come nigh thee.
Only with thine eyes shalt thou
behold
and see the reward of the wicked.
Because thou hast made the Lord,
which is my refuge,
even the Most High, thy habituation;
there shall no evil befall thee,
neither shall any plague come nigh
thy dwelling.
For he shall give his angels charge
over thee,
to keep thee in all thy ways.
They shall bear thee up in their
Hands,
lest thou dash thou foot against a
stone.
Thou shalt treat upon the lion and
adder:
the young lion and the dragon shalt
thou trample under feet.
Because he hath set his love upon
me, therefore will I deliver him:
I will set him on high, because he
hath known my name.
He shall call upon me, and I will
answer Him:
I will be with him in trouble;
I will deliver him and honor him.
With long life will I satisfy him,
and show him my salvation."

Psalms 141:8–10

"But my eyes are fixed upon thee, O God: in thee is my trust: leave not my soul destitute. Keep me from the snares that they have laid for me, and the gins of the workers of iniquity. Let the wicked fall into their own nets, whilst that I withal escape."

James 4:4

"Hey you adulterous people, don't you know that friendship of the world is hatred towards God? Anyone who chooses to become a friend of the world becomes an enemy of God."

Psalm 16:8

"I'm always thinking of the LORD; and because He is so near, I never to stumble or fall."

Ephesians 6:10

"Finally, my brethren, be strong in the Lord, and in the power of his might."

Isaiah 41:10

"Fear thou not; for I am with thee: be not dismayed; for I am thy God: I will strengthen thee; yea, I will help thee; yea, I will uphold thee with the right hand of my righteousness."

Proverbs 8:14

"Counsel is mine, and sound wisdom: I am understanding; I have strength."

Fans,

    To all of you who have purchased a copy of this book, I'd like to extend my heartfelt thanks and appreciation for your love and continuous support. Without you, I wouldn't have come this far. Thank you!

Your poet,
Kota J. Franklin

Poetry is the utterance of deep and heartfelt truth. The true poet is very near the oracle.

—Edward Hubbell Chapin

 LIVE

listen|imagine|view|experience

AUDIO BOOK DOWNLOAD INCLUDED WITH THIS BOOK!

In your hands you hold a complete digital entertainment package. In addition to the paper version, you receive a free download of the audio version of this book. Simply use the code listed below when visiting our website. Once downloaded to your computer, you can listen to the book through your computer's speakers, burn it to an audio CD or save the file to your portable music device (such as Apple's popular iPod) and listen on the go!

How to get your free audio book digital download:

1. Visit www.tatepublishing.com and click on the e|LIVE logo on the home page.
2. Enter the following coupon code:
   e26d-bb5b-1843-bf56-6ea7-ec75-7f33-25c4
3. Download the audio book from your e|LIVE digital locker and begin enjoying your new digital entertainment package today!

CPSIA information can be obtained at www.ICGtesting.com
Printed in the USA
BVOW05s2244120916

461908BV00005B/8/P